G000038763

ENGLISH IN THE PRIMARY SCHOOL

TRICIA EVANS

THE AUTHOR

Tricia Evans is a Lecturer in English in Education at the University of Keele. She has taught, and continues to teach, in a number of primary schools, and is the author of Teaching English (Croom Helm, 1982) and Drama in English Teaching (Croom Helm, 1984).

Subjects in the Primary School

Series editor: Professor John Eggleston, University of Warwick

ENGLISH IN THE PRIMARY SCHOOL

TRICIA EVANS

ROUTLEDGE & KEGAN PAUL
LONDON

To R.R.E.

First published in 1987 by
Routledge & Kegan Paul Ltd
11 New Fetter Lane, London EC4P 4EE

Set in 11/12 pt Sabon
by Columns of Reading
and printed in Great Britain
by Cox & Wyman Ltd, Reading

British Library Cataloguing in Publication Data
Evans, Tricia
English in the primary school.——(Subjects in the primary school).
1. English language——Study and teaching
(Elementary)——Great Britain
I. Title II. Series
372.6'044'0941   LB1576
ISBN 0–7102–0781–6

2.99

Contents

1

English and the primary school curriculum

Post 'Plowden': a historical perspective

It is difficult to analyse the role of English in the primary school curriculum without assessing, to some extent at least, the nature and origins of that curriculum. We could turn the curricular clock back to the nineteenth century all-age elementary schools which were only beginning to disappear in 1944, and thus to the 3Rs, standards and payment by results. We might pause at the *Hadow Report*[1] of 1931 which confirmed the need for a break in elementary schooling at the age of 11, and famously stated that 'the curriculum of the primary school is to be thought of in terms of activity and experience, rather than of knowledge to be acquired and facts to be stored'. We would inevitably linger in 1944 to note the implications of the Education Act of that year which led to the introduction of the 11+, and would pause in 1965 to recognize the spur given to the abandonment of this same examination by Antony Crosland's Circular 10/65.

Such a rapid journey through the past might give the erroneous impression that the progress through time had been logically ameliorative, unseating the utilitarian manifestations of the nineteenth century push for mass literacy and demolishing the crude determinism of the psychometrists. But by 1967, the year of publication of the *Plowden Report*,[2] the great majority of 11-year-olds were still sitting the 11+, in schools still dominated by the 3Rs, and the progressive movement led by Froebel, Montessori and McMillan had only effectively reached the children of a middle class elite.

Although the *Plowden Report* built upon the work of its

predecessors and explicitly recognized its debt to the *Hadow Reports* of 1931 and 1933,[3] it can be seen as a watershed publication, since its recommendations went considerably further in advocating child-centred education than previous reports, and since it reached a much greater audience than its predecessors. Those of us training to be primary teachers in the years immediately following its publication were left in no doubt of its impact or importance, and its influence goes on, for no primary teacher today can claim to be unaffected by the *Plowden Report*. It has been described as 'The latest, and certainly most comprehensive and authoritative statement of the principles (or theory) which should govern classroom practice' and 'the backdrop against which schools and teachers have operated now for more than a decade'.[4]

Although the report could not change a great deal (too many of its recommendations had financial implications) it did provide a fillip for a move towards more child-centred, unstreamed education and described an ideal: 'in the Report we have for the most part described English primary education at its best.' And, 'Our review is a report of progress and a spur to more.'[5] Not the least of its achievements was in providing a memorable ideological shorthand which was to permeate the training courses and consciousness (if not always the practice) of the post-Plowden generations of teachers:

Spoken language plays a central role in learning.[6]

The development of language is . . . central to the educational process.[7]

Individual differences between children of the same age are so great that any class, however homogeneous it seems, must always be treated as a body of children needing individual and different attention.[8]

The school sets out deliberately to devise the right environment for children, to allow them to be themselves and to develop in the way and at the pace appropriate to them.[9]

The sense of personal discovery influences the intensity of a child's experience, the vividness of his memory and the probability of effective transfer of learning.[10]

It is easy to assimilate these bald, amputated statements painlessly and uncritically, as some have done in the past. It is easy to see how facile interpretation of these ideological principles can lead to misguided practice where 'spoken language' becomes inconsequential chatter and 'being yourself' amounts to bad behaviour. Many of the *Plowden Report*'s once fresh, even surprising statements have acquired the patina of received wisdom and trip from the tongue as smoothly as slogans:

At the heart of the educational process lies the child.[11]

The child is the agent in his own learning.[12]

In part this is a result of the crusading optimism of the Plowden committee, but it is also due to the temptation to disregard the report's caveats. The famous statement concerning discovery, quoted above, is in fact heavily qualified:

At the same time it is true that trivial ideas and inefficient methods may be 'discovered'. Furthermore, time does not allow children to find their way by discovery to all that they have to learn. In this matter, as in all education, the teacher is responsible for encouraging children in enquiries which lead to discovery and for asking leading questions.

Far from encouraging a flabby laissez-faire approach in the classroom, the *Plowden Report* recommended a balance:

What is immediately needed is that teachers should bring to bear on their day to day problems astringent intellectual scrutiny. Yet all good teachers must work intuitively and be sensitive to the emotive and imaginative needs of their children.[13]

Turning the clock back in this way is salutory in that it can focus attention on the often anomalous legacy of past practices and misconceptions. All primary schools share a concern with a particular age range, 5 to 11, and a belief in the concept of the class teacher. Both are the result of historical accident and bureaucratic pragmatism. The class teacher is as organizationally

3

and financially expedient today as she was in the nineteenth century elementary schools. She effectively provides a total educational package on the cheap. The fact that later commentators underpinned the class teacher system with a persuasive rationale does not alter the fact that today's class teachers follow directly in the footsteps of their Victorian counterparts. Similarly, the choice of 5 as the age for beginning school was made almost casually in 1870, as elementary education for all was introduced; while the current notion of 11 as the watershed age came about as a convenient midpoint between elementary and secondary schooling at a time when the majority of pupils left school at or before the age of 14. The importance of 11 as a major transitional point in the pupil's career was of course later reinforced by Cyril Burt's false assumption that long-term intellectual potential could be foreseen at this early age.

Recent research[14] focuses attention on yet another apparent unifying principle in primary education, and another legacy from the past: a belief in the supremacy of the 'basic skills' of reading, writing and arithmetic. Despite the educational insecurities of the 1970s, publicized through Jim Callaghan's 1976 Ruskin College speech and the 'Back to Basics' lobby, it would seem that the 3Rs, once so crucially important in educating an innumerate and illiterate future electorate, have maintained their curricular dominance through the prestige accorded to them in today's primary classrooms. Both the 1978 and 1982 DES primary surveys[15] note that this concentration on the 3Rs is inevitably at the cost of the remainder of the curriculum.

Implicit in the notion of the importance of the 3Rs is the idea that the primary school curriculum can be conveniently divided between, not merely reading, writing and arithmetic, but all else besides. The backwash from the early grammar schools' classical curriculum of clearly defined subjects remains and permeates the language of educational discourse. Even those teachers who practise the truly integrated day and believe in the seamless robe of learning often define pupil practice and progress in conventional subject terms. The *Plowden Report* insisted that knowledge does not divide into neatly separate compartments and yet used subject headings to describe aspects of the curriculum. We may believe that the primary curriculum should be an organic whole but categorization is inevitable if analysis is not to become impossibly nebulous.

Organizational models for the teaching of English

What then is 'English' and what is its place in the primary school curriculum? A statement of whole school aims of the kind advocated by the Schools Council[16] suggests something of this relationship:

In setting its whole school aims, for example, a primary school might wish each of its pupils to learn

(i) to read fluently and accurately, with understanding, feeling and discrimination;

(ii) to develop a legible style of handwriting and satisfactory standards of spelling, syntax, punctuation and usage;

(iii) to communicate clearly and confidently in speech and writing, in ways appropriate for various occasions and purposes;

(iv) to listen attentively and with understanding;

(v) to learn how to acquire information from various sources, and to record information and findings in various ways;

(vi) to apply computational skills with speed and accuracy;

(vii) to understand the applications of mathematical ideas in various situations in home, classroom, school and local area;

(viii) to observe living and inanimate things, and to recognize characteristics such as pattern and order;

(ix) to master basic scientific ideas;

(x) to investigate solutions and interpret evidence, to analyse and to solve problems;

(xi) to develop awareness of self and sensitivity to others, acquire a set of moral values and the confidence to make and hold to moral judgments, and develop habits of self-discipline and acceptable behaviour;

(xii) to know about geographical, historical and social aspects of the local environment and the national heritage, to be aware of other times and places, and to recognize links between local, national and international events;

(xiii)   to acquire sufficient control of self or of tools, equipment and instruments to be able to use music, drama and several forms of arts and crafts as means of expression;

(xiv)   to develop agility and physical coordination, confidence in and through physical activity, and the ability to express feeling through movement.

English helps to fulfil all these aims at three different levels: firstly, at the subject-specific level indicated in aims (i) to (iv), which English will claim as particularly its own; secondly, at the 'language across the curriculum' level English will help to achieve aims (v), (x), (xi) and (xiii). Thirdly, as the medium for learning, English will inevitably contribute to the fulfilment of all the remaining aims. It is significant that, as so often in this kind of school list, language aims predominate at the top, perhaps in recognition of the perceived importance of English in the curriculum, and the likelihood that English activities will have the greatest share of curricular time.

English as a curricular area will subsume reading, writing, talking and listening. The order of importance primary teachers attach to these in practice will depend upon a number of factors, most notably the perceived needs and abilities of the pupils, and the quality of the environment and resources. Thus there will be less pressure to test successful spellers, and an intensive reading week may be encouraged by a 'book flood'. It is an educational truism that it is not what teachers say but what they do, not theory but practice, which truly defines their interpretation of teaching. Hence different approaches to English are best revealed, not by eloquent statements of intent, but by witnessing the course of events in the classroom. The portraits of individual primary classes which follow attempt to go some way towards achieving this by freezing teacher and pupils at significant moments:

Model 1 Infants, 6 to 7 years, box classroom (see Figure 1.1)

It is difficult to generalize about what the children are doing. Not all of them are immediately visible; two are sitting on the carpeted area known as the Book Corner, looking at picture books and trying to find examples of kinds of insects. In the

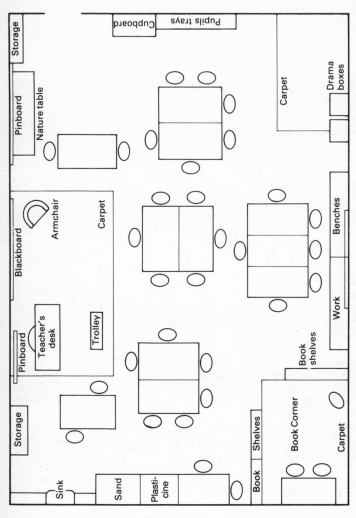

Figure 1.1

process they are attempting to classify the creatures they find: 'No, that's not an insect because . . . .' They are about to seek out the teacher to ask how many legs insects have.

Two pupils are weighing beakers of sand on a simplified scale. The teacher has asked them whether they think wet sand is heavier than dry sand and then to test their hypothesis. Several pupils are erratically finishing their section of a class frieze, which has as its theme 'A Day at the Seaside'. Each of the drawings will be accompanied by a brief description. Two of the pupils are copying the teacher's version of their oral suggestions; several more are laboriously writing without the teacher's aid and another has her hand up since she cannot find the right crayon.

Two children who have just completed their contribution to the frieze are tidying up the drama boxes in the corner, since their contents have been used during playtime. They are talking as they do it, in part to give each other instructions, and in part to eke out the task, since they relish their independence beyond the sight line of the teacher. Another child is searching in his locker and another is retrieving a pencil which has rolled under the tables.

The teacher is intermittently hearing a pupil read. At intervals she straightens her spine and lifts an eyebrow threateningly, to damp down noise or disturbance. She grunts occasionally to the pupil standing at her side, and asks a quick question or two, before beckoning another pupil to the front to read. One child is hovering to her right in order to ask for help since 'My tooth's coming out Miss'. The teacher has not as yet noticed him; her attention is divided between the reader, the remainder of the class and the pupil who has yet to return from the toilet.

The remainder of the class are at least nominally reading. They have finished their frieze work and have taken out their readers. Some children are muttering as they sound out words and follow them with their fingers; two are looking at the pictures in an apparently random manner and one is copying some of the words from the book into her word folder.

Several points, relating to classroom organization for English, are raised by this brief portrait:

1   This is not an English lesson, indeed it is not a lesson in its

formal secondary school sense, and both terms have little meaning for the children who often find it difficult to describe what they have done in a day, let alone define activities in terms of traditional academic distinctions or time slots. Nor does the teacher describe the sum total of these activities as English, but rather as:

> . . . part of a continuum of activities for the individual, which while fulfilling my objectives, only have any overall coherence in retrospect. At the end of the day or week say, I try to look back and see the range of work from the point of view of individual children in the class. Have they done enough talking or done too much quiet listening? Have I given them enough attention? What progress have they made in reading or writing? It's all checks and balances, somehow keeping all the plates up in the air . . . .

Thus language practice serves and is served by work which would traditionally be described as art, empirical science, entomology, mathematics, study skills and interpersonal relationships.

2   In this model play and work are not poles apart, the two ends of the home–school dichotomy, but are intertwined. For the children using beakers and a tipper truck in the sand area, this is play in the sense that it is fun, interesting, tactile and messy and has connotations of playgrounds and beaches. They have no formal notion of volume or weight but they are, ideally, building the conceptual basis for the accommodation of such terms later. For these pupils the talk is incidental, an almost unconscious accompaniment to what they are doing with their hands. For the teacher, such talk may be the most significant and planned-for product of the activity.

Similarly, the preparation for and clearing up after an activity may be almost as important as the activity itself since it is in these 'paratask' moments that children's communication and social skills are being developed and tested. The children who have been asked to tidy up the drama boxes have been challenged to negotiate and cooperate in the interests of the whole class. Such a task is part of the pattern of developing personal responsibility and autonomy.

3   For good and ill, some of the learning will not have been anticipated by the teacher's objectives for her pupils, in part because she is also learning: 'Let me tell you, please Miss . . . I know about engines . . . ,' 'Helen would like to show us how you'd make a float.' Of course, in such instances, the pupil is significantly learning too, realizing that his or her experiences count in the classroom, that he or she can make a contribution to the curriculum or alter the course of the session. In such circumstances the pupil is crystallizing and collating information, fixing it in time and space, making the ephemeral more permanent so that it can be reflected upon, made memorable by its place in a particularly vivid scene, and by the delight of being the centre of attention, the expert.

Children may stumble upon a challenge which the teacher's plans have not anticipated: 'Why doesn't that fly fall off the ceiling Miss?' 'Why's Gerald got to have a sweet?' In so doing they may also be stumbling upon the language required to frame the hypothetical: 'But if we make it bigger it won't go through.' The teacher may be totally unaware of some of the learning taking place in the classroom and some of the uses to which language is put in the hidden curriculum. The 'sub-text' of the lesson may include those furtive threats, promises, requests and secrets which cumulatively indicate a pupil's pecking order in the class.

4   The children in this example are not being taught as a class but are involved in a number of activities, thus the teacher can, so long as she is vigilant, concentrate on the work of a sub-group, however temporarily. Groups form, divide, coalesce in a fluid yet generally rational fashion. Sometimes the rationale will be the teacher's: 'Move over to work with Gary, you'll have more room there,' 'Now you people missed our work with shapes didn't you?' and sometimes the children's: 'Can I play with Laura? I've got my hat.' In line with the *Plowden Report*'s recommendations, these groupings are not allowed to become fossilized. While pupils may go to their home base table at transitional moments in the day, and while they may cling possessively to their best friends, they will work with all the other members of the class in the course of a week.

5   The role of the teacher of infants is clearly different from that of the teacher of older junior pupils. The former is inevitably more akin to the nursery teacher in that her pastoral role is more apparent. Where the teacher of top juniors or secondary teacher is more aware of the academic-pastoral divide, the teacher of infants will see these two as an indivisible whole: the child who has gone to the toilet may be following a routine procedure to return promptly with trousers fastened and hands washed. But he is just as likely to encounter a problem: 'There's a big puddle in there,' 'I can see a spider.' More seriously, the trip may be seen against a background of family problems; the child cannot cope when going to the toilet alone perhaps because of a fear of dark places or because of an unpleasant incident at home.

Such apparently routine events are probably more memorable, more centre stage for the child than many of the planned learning activities. A child does not quickly forget the moment when the class stops work to witness the teacher tucking in a wayward shirt while delivering an embarrassing reprimand, and the emotional fall-out from such a spectacle can colour all that the child does in the course of that day or week and, if repeated, may fuel a long-lasting grudge or introversion which causes the child to keep as mute as possible for days, rather than engage riskily in conversation with the teacher.

6   Many calls are made on the teacher and she must be aware of how she divides her time between individuals. Children may use diversionary tactics to draw attention to themselves, their boredom, their insecurity. These may range from the fictional wobbly tooth of the example to one hundred and one ways to waste time when waiting for teacher or collecting materials. In the course of any session the teacher will act as organizer, instructor, observer, nursing auxiliary, guide, umpire and confidant. She cannot say, as the secondary teacher might, 'Now get on in silence for the next ten minutes,' or 'No more questions, you'll have to sort out the problems for yourselves.'

7   There is inevitably quite a large degree of movement in the classroom, movement between activities as children move from one area or group to another, within activities as they

11

collect or return material or seek help. The teacher will be the most peripatetic member of the class, only seated for good reason, otherwise moving around the classroom to inquire, encourage, redirect, listen and respond. The noise level may at times be quite high, since much of the 'English' consists of oral language, rather than the more solitary reading and writing. Nevertheless, there will be oases of quiet when the noise level falls, because the teacher requests it, the work demands it or in specified areas, for example, the Book Corner.

Of course, such a freeze-frame view does not constitute the whole picture of English work in this infants classroom. It significantly does not and cannot describe the lesson from the point of view of every child, for any one perspective will be unique, part of a kaleidoscopic pattern which constitutes the total experiences of the lesson. It also fails to take account of the fact that the organizational model frozen here is merely one of many to be found in this classroom at different times in the week. If we turn the clock on by four hours we will find the whole class grouped around the teacher for 'Story Time'. If we turn the clock back by two hours we would witness the teacher questioning the class about the Bible story they had heard in Assembly, before setting the children off on their various tasks.

Model 2 Juniors, 9 to 11 years, semi-open plan classroom (see Figure 1.2), designed for team teaching across the age range.

This second model, like the first, suggests the possible breadth of any interpretation of English. Here an explanatory preamble is needed before the classes are frozen in action. In this case the work is nominally more circumscribed since pupils are all working simultaneously on aspects of the same project. 'The Countryside', which is introduced through group visits to mixed farms in the area. While small groups may form for remedial work in an aspect of English, most of the English activities emerge from the reading, writing and discussion associated with the project.

A relevant book display is set out in the library area and pupils are encouraged to bring in their own exhibits. This

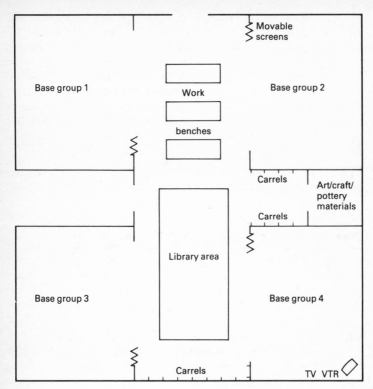

Figure 1.2

project has proved very successful in the past and the teachers have amassed a considerable range of audio-visual and display materials. The work is underpinned by a study skills programme, begun in the first year junior class, which helps pupils to 'research' with some confidence and flexibility. The older children, who are more familiar with this kind of project work, are in a position to help the younger children, particularly when it comes to identifying the possibilities for individual inquiry topics. Thus, following the farm visits, all pupils are asked to subdivide the theme into manageable sections. This may come about through rough notes, with the help of reference books, or through discussion, or through a combination

13

of all three. The children are asked to record their conclusions diagrammatically, in any way they think appropriate.

On this afternoon, two weeks after the beginning of the project, all the children have been listening to a nun from the local convent describing her experiences of farming in England and Zambia. Many pupils are fascinated that this statuesque figure should ever have looped up her habit to feed chickens and goats. They question their visitor sensibly, as they have previous visitors. There is no requirement that the children write about such talks, although some choose to do so. By a quarter to two all the children are engaged in a variety of mainly self-chosen tasks, many of which continue work begun the day before.

One group of children is being helped by a student teacher to edit a tape recording of farmyard sounds. He suggests that they might consider expressing these onomatopoeically on paper, with relevant illustrations, for display. The group prefers however to plan for the collection of village sounds. Two children are modelling different kinds of ovens in clay; they will contribute to the 'Cooking around the World' display. Many pupils are working from library books which have been reserved temporarily for their use; two are quarrelling since they are competing for the same texts. The teacher responsible for their area wonders whether to intervene to resolve the conflict, or whether they are better left to negotiate a *modus operandi* for themselves.

Two children are calculating the relative proportions of land allotted to livestock and crops in the farm they have recently visited. Two more are devising a board game, provisionally called 'Farming Millionaire', which is based upon their understanding of farming practices and problems, and includes Chance cards: 'Underinsured barn burns down. Lose £3,000,' 'Government pays you not to drain a marsh. Gain £5,000.' They are testing the instructions on the uninitiated, to assess whether or not they are foolproof. Three children are dressing cardboard figures with their own interpretations of the clothes worn by nineteenth century shepherds and dairymaids. They are about to write about a typical day in the life of both.

Several pupils are trying to make sense of an Ordnance Survey map of the local area. A teacher is listening to their comments and is hoping that they will come to identify the relationship between contours, rivers and settlements. Other children are scanning a facsimile of an eighteenth century map of the county. A larger group is tucked quietly in a corner of Base Area One; the children are working on their chosen sub-theme, 'The Village of Prince's Norton'. It is an imaginary village, based upon their researches into the medieval agricultural community. The teacher has suggested that they consider a cast list as one possible starting point and the children are rapidly identifying with their chosen character roles and are planning to bring the village to life through drama.

A gradually increasing audience of pupils is watching one of ITV's 'History Around You' series. This programme considers what can be deduced about the history of the countryside from the present day appearance of fields and villages. The children stop the tape at intervals in order to allow time for discussion and note making. Two children are entering 'Work Completed' into their work profile sheets. Several others are waiting to catch the attention of the relevant teacher in order to have their work checked. A larger group is making vocabulary charts to accompany those already displayed in the area. Some concentrate on key figures in the countryside, both at home and abroad; others are listing vocabulary by parts of speech, including the adjectives deemed most appropriate for certain animals and the verbs which describe the processes involved in bread making. Some children have already progressed to a more poetic extension of this, devising enigmatic riddle poems with the collective titles 'Who am I?' and 'What am I?'

Since the afternoon is fine two pupils have been given permission to take their work outside. All the art and craft tables have been commandeered and they require ample space in which to design their maypole and decide the pattern the dancers must follow if the ribbons are to combine in a coherent manner. Four other pupils are also outside, undertaking an ecological survey of the flora and fauna of the playing field.

What conclusions can we draw from this brief portrait? As with the first example, it is clear that English is not explicitly singled out from the rest of the curriculum. While one of the four teachers is the language postholder and, where necessary, fulfils the role of remedial teacher of English, there is not an English language text book in sight, since the staff prefer to explore language use in the context of pupils' own, ideally self-chosen, work. The children are not called to the front to read to their teacher, partly because there is no front in the usual sense, teachers are too peripatetic for that, but more significantly because pupils are encouraged to read to each other and to read their work aloud to the teacher, when appropriate. The latter is seen as having a diagnostic purpose while also encouraging children to identify obvious mistakes in their own work. This sporadic reading practice is reinforced by timetabled library periods when the teachers have less disturbed opportunities for monitoring pupils' reading progress and interests.

It is clear that this project model for the teaching of English demands careful appraisal of pupils' work if they are not to waste time and are to cover a suitable range of reading, writing and discussion activities. There is a danger of too much unsupervised copying from books and a risk of too much inconsequential chatter, where pupils feel they are out of range of the teacher. There is also the danger that the interesting range of activities taking place simultaneously may distract the most impressionable children from their own work, or allow insufficient sanctuaries for those children who need peace and quiet in which to concentrate.

This kind of model for the teaching of English can only succeed where staff are willing to work hard to prepare for, and follow up, a wide range of pupil work. Such a range is only feasible where children have been carefully introduced to this distinctive way of working. The model would inevitably break down if pupils could not exploit the library confidently, if they failed to show consideration for others or if they habitually turned to a teacher to answer every query, however trivial. It could not work if the more retiring children were neglected in the teachers' anxiety to cope with the discipline problems posed by the small minority of more aggressive and extrovert children. Thus good relationships and control are arguably even more vitally important in this open plan area than they would be in the traditional box classroom with a less heterogeneous ability and age range. Clearly, too, the project model should never be allowed to stifle pupil initiative and choice; there should still be opportunities for children to follow up topical local or national events or pursue tangential inquiries of their own.

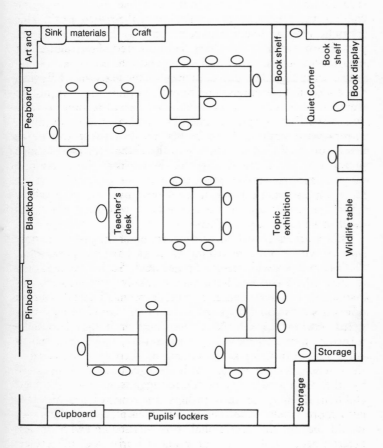

Figure 1.3

Model 3 Juniors, 7 to 8 years, box classroom
(see Figure 1.3)

Here, as often in junior classes, the children are accustomed to belonging to a number of groups, for different purposes: the base group in which they begin and often end the day and undertake music, drama, gym and any other whole class activities; the curriculum 'sets' commonly used for language and mathematics work; and ephemeral groups employed where, for example, a lack of resources may mean that not all the children can attempt tie dying simultaneously. Thus, if challenged, a child might claim membership of Mr Jones's first year class, but might also belong to the red set for mathematics and the yellow group for English. These sets may have everything or nothing to do with ability. In the former case, pupils may quickly and shrewdly deduce where they are in the ability stakes from the number on the language text book, the colour of the comprehension workcard and the calibre of the company. More insidiously, the teacher's comments or attention may define her perception of a child's ability. Where groups are not determined by ability then they may act as a guarantee of curricular diversity and balance where, for example, there is a cycle of work and children move from one sub-area to another.

These first year juniors are accustomed to the notion that English and Mathematics will precede dinner while 'topic', art and craft and games are likely to follow it. The morning-to-morning pattern is decided by the timetable for schools broadcasts, by the teacher's assessment of the needs and moods of her pupils and by local events: the longer than usual assembly which makes silent reading or reading with teacher a sensible option until playtime; the unexpected availability of a parent to help with reading or mathematics; or simply the fact that a pupil has raised an interesting question or brought in an interesting article. The children are used to working as members of one of five groups which contain a spread of ability in the hope that the more able children will be able to help the less able without being held back themselves. The group are labelled with the names of those pupils from each who are responsible for distributing and collecting materials that week.

On this morning, immediately following assembly, each of the groups is continuing with the English work they started the previous day. Steven's group is using English textbooks; working individually or in pairs children are devising a story to accompany a set of cartoons. Karen and Alastair's groups, working in pairs, and having made selections from a set of photographs, are trying to compose a short dialogue based on each. They have been encouraged to discuss and try out the lines before committing them to paper. One pair of pupils, sharing the same photographs, has already decided to work independently, writing everything down before comparing versions to see which they prefer. Another couple has decided to work with one as scribe and another as composer and is eager to tape the finished work. Michael's group is completing its list of words which make the 'ee/ea' sound; their tables are littered with dictionaries. When they have finished their lists they will break into pairs to draft sentences or stories which contain as many of the words as possible. Two members of the group are keen to use some of the words as starting points for charades for performance to the rest of the class. Linda's group is huddled in the Quiet Corner, listening to a truncated tape recorded story; they have been asked to devise at least one convincing ending for this and record their suggestions in writing and perhaps on tape.

Although the English work in this classroom is more limited in range than in the two previous examples, the teacher is no less 'on call' than her infant and team teaching colleagues. On occasions she will deliberately sit down at her desk to help an individual but for much of the time she moves round the classroom as unobtrusively as possible, checking work, asking questions, sharing a joke as she goes. Those children who finish work satisfactorily before the rest of the group will either be pointed towards a suitable reward for their success, perhaps reading a self-chosen book or illustrating the work they have completed, or will be invited to suggest what they would like to do next. If we turn the clock on to the following day, two of the groups will have moved on to another group activity, either one from the original cycle or one devised by the teacher or pupils, while the remainder will be at different stages in the completion of their work.

Clearly, there have to be good reasons for dividing the work and the class up in this way, for groups in themselves do not guarantee collaboration or discussion and can encourage that fragmentation of the English curriculum which leads to fits and starts of ill-assorted work, bemused children and a teacher who does little more than hurry, poorly prepared, from one group to another. Where however groups are exploited for collaborative work, to encourage that cohesion which comes about when children see themselves as specialists in a particular area, or to make the best possible use of limited resources, they amply repay the teacher time and effort which is required if pupils' needs are to be met and suitable materials are to be collected or prepared.

Model 4 Juniors, 10 to 11 years, mobile classroom (see Figure 1.4)

The local weekly newspaper has challenged children to describe and illustrate an invention which they consider would make life more interesting or comfortable in the next century. The teacher wishes to exploit this opportunity but anticipates that, while the children may have some immediate ideas, they will need to be helped and challenged if these are to be imaginatively developed. One of the English periods in the timetable falls on a Tuesday afternoon, after playtime and after drama in the hall. The teacher intends to use the drama session to focus on the theme of 'Inventions'.

The teacher begins the drama session by telling the class that they must listen intently to what he is about to say. He proceeds to describe the detailed workings of a bicycle pump, without naming it and using the first person 'I'. Pupils are asked to suggest what is being described, quoting particular pieces of evidence. They are then asked to prepare their own oral descriptions of well-known inventions for the benefit of their partners who must deduce what is being described. The teacher asks the children to imagine that they are the promoter of their invention and that they are trying to persuade a manufacturer to mass produce it. They are asked to consider the distinctive characteristics of their invention and to anticipate the questions the manufacturer may ask. This leads into a piece of improvised drama where each pair acts out the scene which portrays the first meeting of inventor and manufacturer. The teacher asks the children to imagine the same scene in the year 2050 and to think of inventions which may be needed then.

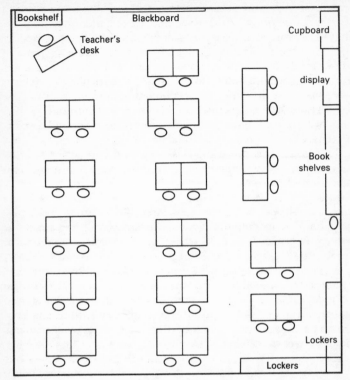

Figure 1.4

The class repeats the process as before, acting out their scenes in front of an audience which is invited to pose supplementary questions to manufacturer or inventor. This completes the hour's work prior to the afternoon break; the class has no choice but to return to their classroom, since the hall will be needed for a gym session.

At the moment when the final afternoon session is frozen, the class is seated, as normally, in a pattern familiar in the secondary school but rarer in primary schools, in pairs at desks which have been pushed together. Unlike all three earlier examples, the class is simultaneously engaged in the same task, producing a written account of a twenty-first century invention.

The teacher has introduced the competition brief and is using this and the preceding drama activities to stimulate original thought and precise descriptions. Some children are approaching the work as a joint assignment from the beginning, pooling ideas which both write down; some are writing independently in the first instance before comparing accounts. Several children have begun with a rough draft diagram of their invention; a few are looking at pictures of Heath Robinson contraptions and two children have expressed disappointment that suitable materials are not readily at hand for making their invention.

The teacher has asked the class to get on without help for as long as possible since he needs time in which to devise his own invention, thus he is seated at his desk. The classroom is almost silent, apart from the rustling of pages, the scraping of chairs and the whispers of those who are collaborating with their neighbours. One pupil has gone to his locker and two are about to return books to the shelves. The work and conditions of work are of a type to be found in many a secondary school English department, and if we turn the clock on by twenty-five minutes the secondary analogy continues to hold true. The noise level has risen, many pupils have moved from drawing to writing, and vice versa, but all the children are still engaged in the same task. There is no stopping early for a story and less time is given to 'clearing up' than in previous examples. The teacher draws the class together only to anticipate where the work will lead, 'into best', to display and competition entry.

The four models illustrated above suggest the range of organizational and teaching methods, and thus role options, open to the teacher of English in the primary school. He or she may, in response to changing circumstances, become nurse, instructor, co-worker, audience, consultant or director, from minute to minute, from one pupil to another. These frozen portraits are indications of what does happen, rather than exemplary or cautionary paradigms, and they demonstrate that, despite the range of interpretations, all primary teachers of English share a concern for pupil generation of and response to spoken and written language. The examples range from the informal integrated model which is closer to the child-centred, individualized end of the ideological spectrum, via the semi-integrated 'topic' approach, to the traditional differentiated model which sees English as a distinct curriculum slot in which whole class teaching methods dominate. A glance at the timetables for individual classes may immediately suggest something of the implicit or explicit importance accorded to English and indicate something of the teacher's general teaching philosophy. The teacher who believes in the more integrated child-centred model will feel that a whole class timetable is rendered meaningless by the emphasis placed on meeting the needs and interests of individual children, as they arise. She may carry in her head the times of whole class games sessions, or broadcasts, but will otherwise envisage not one but many timetables, each describing the balance of activities for any one child in the class. Conversely, the final example of a class of top juniors emerges from a formal timetable where English and drama appear at set times throughout the week and term.

The four examples do not exhaust the possible organizational models for the teaching of English in the primary school. They do not include a description of pure and inevitably rare programmed learning where each child follows a sequence of work, in isolation, tailored neatly to his own needs (conceivably with the aid of a computer in the future). They do not include a portrait of a single class rural primary school nor a description of a classroom in which the child's mother tongue and English have equal importance; nor do they pretend to represent the whole story of how these teachers choose to organize English. They may move in and out of models from session to session, month to month, age group to age group. By freezing these examples we are also freezing a particular set of individuals, teachers and children. The content of the lessons will effectively be determined, in part, by the group dynamics of mood, interests and behaviour of those individuals. Primary teachers can be heard to mutter to their colleagues, 'I'd like to do marbling with them but they're not up to it,' 'I don't think we'll have the debate after wet playtime . . .' or 'Now things have settled down at home a bit perhaps he'll show a bit more interest in reading.'

The four models inevitably do not identify how these interpretations of English came about, often as the result of a complex and ultimately indefinable blend of influences derived from the past, the present and aspirations for the future. The blend will include some or all of the following influential factors:

23

1 Head teacher's or other teacher's advice/directive/document.
2 Advisor's or inspector's advice/directive/document.
3 Class teacher's list of longer-term aims or localized objectives.
4 Relevant reading matter other than the above.
5 Implicit or explicit demands of society (parents, local community, employers, media, educational experts).
6 Recognition of the needs, abilities and interests of pupils.
7 Nature of the learning environment.
8 Class teacher's personal expertise, philosophy, confidence and interests.
9 Impact of the initial training and in-service courses.
10 Class teacher's experience as a pupil or as a teacher in other contexts.

Trying to lay bare why we do what we do as teachers of English is particularly important for the primary school teacher, who still retains a great deal of classroom autonomy in a sector where curriculum areas often blur in a way made impossible by most secondary school timetables. While English will be a particularly unquantifiable concept for younger children, it may, dangerously, be almost as amorphous an entity for the teacher. Exposing the pedigree of common primary practices is no simple matter, as Robin Alexander[17] has demonstrated, and even where we try to pinpoint the source: 'I'm doing it this way because that's the only way the resources allow,' our explanation may be dishonest, a smoke-screen rather than a statement of fact. We may slip, politician-like, into circuitous retrospective justification: 'I've always done it this way because that's the way we always do it.' This may be paraphrased as, 'I have my doubts about this method but the Head's prepared to resource this programme,' or 'Anything for a quiet life.' We may be seduced by our own rhetoric: 'This way all the children can develop at their own pace,' 'This school aims to extend pupils' horizons through open-ended inquiries into areas of their own choosing.' Our rationale for the teaching of English, which may have little to do with the bland set of whole school aims recycled each year in the official school handbook, needs to be ruthlessly scrutinized if the anomalous practices of the past are not to become sanctified by time and familiarity alone: 'What must be ensured is that the decisions taken in schools spring from the best available knowledge and are not simply dictated by habit or convention.'[18]

Primary teachers commonly emphasize the importance of encouraging communication and social skills in their pupils, but there is little point in stating such generalized aims if we then fail to determine feasible strategies for achieving them. Designing and evaluating such strategies is no simple or quick matter; it necessitates a series of ongoing teacher analyses of the kind described by Joan Dean,[19] which attempt to answer the questions: What are my aims for these children? How can I help to achieve these long-term aims by translating them into short-term objectives for individual pupils? How can I help to achieve these objectives through the management of learning, through the optimum use of time, the environment, resources and grouping patterns? How can I create a social climate in the classroom in which learning can flourish? How can I help to ensure that all children are being offered the best possible opportunities to make progress in all aspects of the social and academic curriculum? How will I know if or when I have achieved all this? What will I do if I fail?

This is, of course, not a once and for all activity, but should be part of a continual process of review and evaluation.[20] It would be reassuring to be able to quote a definitive blueprint for perfect aims, perfect objectives and exemplary practice in English teaching, but such a statement would fail to take account of the needs of particular pupils, the expertise of particular teachers and the local context in which the learning is taking place. It would also be dangerously restrictive, setting unnecessary perimeters for a fruitfully broad curriculum area. The generally hostile response to the recent HMI attempt to produce just such a statement of perfect English objectives for 7- and 11-year-olds is in part an instinctive reaction to any curriculum straitjacket. Once the official imprimatur is given to such an inadequately annotated list of mechanistic objectives, it is tempting for the less confident and competent teacher to strive for the achievement of these objectives alone, in an equally mechanistic manner. Clearly, though, some notions of good practice are essential if English is not to become neglected in the 'secret garden' of the curriculum. We can conclude that the successful teacher of English will:

1 Understand how children acquire language.[21]
2 Know her children well, monitoring their progress in reading, writing, talking (and listening) continuously and carefully.
3 Manage the curriculum and the classroom in such a way as to ensure that all pupils have opportunities to practise a wide and constructive range of language uses.
4 Help children to enjoy reading, writing and talking so that they come to practise each with confidence.
5 Relate classroom English learning to the wider context of other activities and cultures, both within and beyond school.
6 Help pupils to develop more autonomous control over their own learning, for example through the confident use of study skills.
7 Help pupils to develop the social skills which will lead to sensitivity, consideration and the ability to work successfully with others.
8 Demonstrate flexibility in the use of teaching and grouping strategies, matching these to objectives, the needs of the children and the demands of the context.

2

Reading for meaning

Reading: recent surveys

'Primary Education in England'[1] (1978)

This survey of 542 primary schools noted the 'high degree of priority'[2] accorded to the teaching of basic reading skills, and found that the reading scheme tended to monopolize the reading curriculum at the expense of more interesting and diverse reading materials:

> In almost all the classes there were some opportunities for children to select books for themselves. However, even by the age of eleven, this was given a high enough priority in only about two-fifths of the classes.[3].

Higher-order reading and study skills, including skimming and scanning strategies, were apparently neglected:

> The teaching of these more advanced skills did not occur in three-quarters of 11 year old classes and even in the remaining quarter there was seldom planned and regular practice.[4]

Even more seriously, 'in only a very small minority of classes at any age were children discussing the books they had read at other than a superficial level of comprehension.'[5]

'Extending Beginning Reading'[6] (1981)

The Schools Council 'Extending Beginning Reading' project focused its classroom survey upon 7- to 9-year-old average readers in the first two years of junior education, in an attempt to discover how the early, infant reading skills were consolidated and extended in the two vital but 'neglected' years which followed. The survey discovered that 'the vast majority of teachers in first- and second-year junior classes base their reading teaching on a reading scheme or schemes'[7] and that 'listening to individual children reading was clearly regarded by all teachers as the backbone for their teaching and monitoring of reading'.[8] Most teachers, it appeared, regularly spent between twenty and forty minutes a day listening to their pupils reading their reading scheme books. Not surprisingly teachers had to work very hard in order to hear a large number of children read at this rate, and 'One result of this was that the time devoted to listening to any one child reading aloud was minimal, frequently being no more than thirty seconds per child.'[9] What this can imply in classroom practice is memorably described in the project report account of a twenty-minute lesson period:

> All the children were engaged in activities, such as reading, writing, answering questions or drawing, connected with their basic reading books. The teacher was sitting at her table and calling out individual children to read to her. Other children continued to ask the teacher's help with spelling or other queries. In other words, it was the kind of period which forms a regular feature of the majority of first-year junior classes . . . in this same 20-minute period, the teacher had contact with 18 children. In nine cases she was listening to a child reading, while nine other children came to show written work or ask for help. Most of the contacts with individual children were of 30 seconds or less. The longest contact was of two-and-a-half minutes – with one interruption. While the teacher was working at this terrific pace, at least one girl, and possibly other children, had not done anything likely to improve her reading.[10]

This survey confirmed earlier research findings that primary age children have too little scope for extended self-chosen reading, and discovered that those lucky enough to have such opportunities were likely to be the most able children or better readers who were rewarded for the early completion of tasks with personal reading. Yet again, there was little evidence of any serious attempts to develop higher-order reading skills: 'Much of the comprehension work was based on text books, and was of an elementary kind, involving the answering of factual questions by the selection of words or phrases from the text.'[11] In short, children were, it seemed, seldom challenged to move beyond literal comprehension, to infer, hypothesize or evaluate.

Despite the teachers' belief that the children enjoyed reading aloud to them, three-quarters of those surveyed said that they preferred to read quietly to themselves rather than out loud to their teacher. Many children distinguished clearly between the pleasurable reading they did at home and the functional and tedious reading demanded of them in the classroom. The research report concluded:

> A lesson in which a teacher listens to large numbers of individual children reading aloud to her, for only a brief period each, while other children are supposed to be reading or writing – and constantly interrupting her to ask for help with spellings – does not provide a peaceful atmosphere in which children can become absorbed in their reading or in which teachers can undertake diagnosis or engage in interesting discussions about books with the children.[12]

'Education 5 to 9'[13] (1982)

This survey of eighty first schools in England found reading standards to be 'satisfactory' in approximately three-quarters of the schools but noted:

> In almost all schools the youngest children were introduced too quickly to published reading schemes and phonic practice, with the result that some were confused and made little progress.[14]

There was an 'unduly prolonged concentration on the basic

reading scheme, especially for the able readers who should have been extending their skills while reading more demanding books of reference and fiction.'[15] Almost all the schools apparently lacked guidelines for the extension of reading skills. It is difficult to reconcile the finding that reading standards were satisfactory with the survey's observation that 'The children spent a great deal of time decoding print with the result that they read mechanically and with little understanding of, or interest in, the content'.[16] If children can neither understand nor take any pleasure in what they are reading they can hardly be described as 'satisfactory' readers. It seems that in only a small number of schools did children become engrossed in books. The majority of classes in the survey were criticized for failing to exploit the resources of the school or classroom Book Corner: 'Sadly it was exceptional to find active encouragement for children to borrow both library books and other books from the age of five,'[17] and the survey found classes where no discussion took place, even concerning the books in the reading scheme which formed the total reading experience of the children. The report suggested that teachers' own enthusiasm for books could be infectious and that 'Enjoyment of and enthusiasm for reading were further increased in schools where the children had ample opportunity for browsing and reading, but in three quarters of the schools such opportunities were limited'.[18]

Implications

The results of these surveys alone would suggest that despite the huge amount of teacher attention allotted to the teaching of reading, and despite the fact that children do learn to read, if only in the crudely functional sense of graduating from the reading scheme with a reading age of 9, many children are apparently not learning to be readers in the true sense of reading a wide range of self-chosen materials for pleasure and for meaning. It is clear from these surveys that many pupils do not enjoy much of the reading they are asked to do in class and that while, in most cases, they are effeciently decoding the written symbols, many are failing to progress from the graphophonological and syntactic level of 'sounding out' letters and words to the reconciliation of these sounds with semantic reality, based upon their own learning experiences. In short, many are failing to comprehend much of what they are reading, particularly when comprehension moves beyond the literal level. The Bullock committee described it thus: 'The teachers were assiduous in their concern that the child should "learn to read", but when he could decode to their satisfaction they came to see him as self-supporting.'[19]

It is a truism to suggest that all teachers need continually to reappraise their teaching practices. Arguably, this is more important in the case of reading because we commonly allocate so much time and importance to it, because it is seen as the key literary skill by parents and pupils, and because failure to read and comprehend may be irretrievably compounded as the child brands himself as a failure and finds a vital learning medium barred to him. Such a reappraisal might well result, as below, in a list of key teaching principles and strategies which may help to inform future classroom practices. Such a list would sensibly begin with some consideration, necessarily brief here, of the reading process.

The reading process

1 Before children can begin to read they need to understand that writing is meaningful, that is it contains a message which is interesting and which can be unlocked, and that words on the page represent the sounds and thence the meanings familiar to the child through oral language.

2 The novice reader will find it easier to read and understand written material if it conforms to the 'natural' vocabulary and speech patterns he already knows. Thus written language which is not predictable in this colloquial sense will be more difficult to read.

3 Learning to read requires a great deal of application, indeed almost an act of faith and trust that it will all be worthwhile in the end. The child will find reading most valid and pleasurable when it serves his own purposes, whether enjoyment, the search for information, or to complete a self-chosen task.

4 It is in no way 'cheating' for children to read material which they find easy; indeed, they will only be motivated

to read more and more widely if much of what they read is easily accessible.

5 Many children have already met a wide range of written material, even if they have not always comprehended it, before starting school. Parents have a key role, arguably *the* key role, to play in reading development, through showing their children that reading is meaningful and pleasurable, and by reading to and with children in a supportive manner.

6 Decoding, however fluent, is not true reading since the latter always presupposes comprehension. Decoding and comprehension should always go hand in hand; it is not true to suggest, as some have in the past, that decoding can precede comprehension, nor that the acquisition of certain key reading skills (skimming, scanning, reading silently, choosing books) should be postponed until decoding is mastered. These reading strategies should all be practised in the infants classroom. Successful readers are not merely fluent decoders but are independent silent readers who happily choose to read, are capable of choosing what to read, and understand what they read.

7 The child is helped to understand the links between reading and writing by developing both skills simultaneously, for example, through suggesting a statement, writing or copying the words, and reading the words. This process is valuably extended where the words invite a direct response, for example where they constitute a letter which results in a reply from the receiver, which is then read in its turn.

8 All readers, however experienced, sometimes diverge from the text, producing 'miscues' which are not serious if the meaning is not radically impaired. An insistence on total accuracy when the child reads aloud can induce a fear of making mistakes, can inhibit retrospective revision in the light of the context, and can induce a fear of reading *per se*.

9 Reading aloud is merely a means to the goal of helping children to read silently and independently. Reading aloud is a rather artificial reading type, a performance which has all the pressure which is missing when the child reads silently. It is reading 'in best' and tends to put the

emphasis on getting it right first time.

10 Prediction is a fundamental reading skill. The reader makes sense of the text by hypothesizing, by predicting likely meanings, using all the phonic, syntactic and semantic clues available. Thus the reader exploits his existing knowledge of the sound of letters (phonic clues), of how language works (syntactic clues), and of what is likely to follow given his understanding of the localized context, which simultaneously relates to his real life experience of the behaviour of similar objects, creatures, or characters (semantic clues).

11 Children commonly feel that guessing the meaning of a word is wrong, but this is a valuable strategy where the guess is related to the context, and one which all competent readers use when moving fluently through the text.

12 Proficient readers tend not to read through a text non-stop. They are prepared to go back, stop where necessary, pause for thought, compare the text with what goes before or follows and discuss the material, whether newspaper, novel, poem, or reference work.

13 Many children, not unnaturally, see progression or lack of it through the reading scheme as synonymous with success or failure. This is particularly true where only the most proficient readers earn the privilege of choosing their own reading materials.

Organization for reading

1 Reading can only flourish in a classroom climate which positively encourages a wide range of pleasurable language activities.

2 Reading practice should not be equated solely with the 'reader' or reading periods. Children can learn to read by reading anything, advertisements, television graphics, notices, labels, magazines and comics, at any time. By associating reading with fixed times and methods we may give the erroneous impression that reading is only fun when, for example, the teacher does it in 'Story Time'; elsewhere it may amount to little more than a utilitarian

chore as the child plods through the reading scheme in the interests of vocabulary acquisition.

3   Organizational methods which suit the teacher may not always help the child to enjoy and practise reading, thus an insistence that all children sit on chairs, or only read books in a specified difficulty band, may be counter-productive.

4   Children need time and quiet in which to learn to read. The teacher should beware of being over-intrusive when a child is silently and enjoyably reading. Over-intervention can fracture the sense and atmosphere and destroy the child's 'run at' the text.

5   Books are not simply for reading from beginning to end in successive sittings. They may be looked at because of the quality of their illustrations, or for reference purposes; they may be temporarily abandoned, compared with others or discussed. Organization for reading should accommodate all these strategies.

6   No child is ever too old or too sophisticated for listening to an adult reading aloud. 'Story Time' should not be restricted to the infants, nor reserved for the end of the day. It offers the teacher or parent valuable opportunities for unlocking reading material which otherwise children would find too difficult to read unaided, and is an important social activity, particularly where children spend much of their time working alone.

7   The teacher needs to demonstrate her own enthusiasm for reading, by sharing her own reading interests with pupils, and through her expressive reading aloud of a wide range of interesting materials.

8   Reading should not be seen exclusively as a solitary activity; it can be collaborative, thus children may profitably read to or with each other in pairs or groups.

9   As teachers we would do well to make the great imaginative leap into the inexperienced reader's shoes to try to envisage the threat posed by an apparently unintelligible piece of text,[20] particularly when the context is reading to teacher in front of thirty curious spectators.

10 We would do well to ask ourselves (and answer honestly): How do I like to read? How would I want to learn to read if I was beginning now? Almost without exception we

would admit that we would want a pressure-free, non-competitive environment in which to find our reading feet, and one where we would be given time to hypothesize, backtrack and correct the inevitable miscues, while having recourse to a friendly and supportive expert, who would respond to our requests, rather than dragging us into the limelight to perform in public. We would want to give short shrift to any expert who disturbed the flow of meaning in order to correct insignificant omissions or mispronunciations. We would prefer to choose our own books, perhaps comfortingly reading a much-loved book several times over before having the courage to launch into something new. We would want the freedom to pause at length, to think about what we have, and are about to read and would, on occasions, choose to read part of a book, abandon it in favour of another, before returning to our original choice, for perfectly legitimate reasons. We would not choose to attempt to read all materials in the same manner or for the same reasons. At times we would recognize an unsuitable choice and abandon it altogether. This reader-centred approach comes close to that which some fortunate children meet when learning to read with parent or grandparent in their own homes. The best classroom reading arrangements approximate most closely to this intimate and domestic ideal.

Choosing and using reading materials

1 When selecting books for the classroom and library we will balance our aim of providing children with a wide range of good quality reading materials with the purely pragmatic criterion of what actually interests them. Thus, for example, a book which contains sexist or racist overtones (whether in the text or illustrations) will fall at the first hurdle of teacher selection, but one which passes this test may still fail at the hurdle of pupil interest.

2 Children should enjoy looking at and making sense of 'real books' (that is non-reading scheme books) from the very earliest stages of learning to read.

3 Children should have ready access to a wide range of

books, in a wide range of difficulty levels, in the classroom. 'Broad band' labelling of books according to difficulty can be useful if pupils understand the system and if this does not prevent them making apparently inappropriate choices.

4 Children's reading age scores provide little guidance as to which material they will actually enjoy or make sense of, firstly because tests are so often based on word recognition rather than on global comprehension, and secondly because children can make nonsense of their assessed reading ages by choosing and understanding books which really interest them, and which in crude readability score would appear to be too demanding.

5 The good practices common in infant classrooms – the comfortable reading corner, the book trolleys, children's own book displays – should continue throughout the primary years; they should not be allowed to wither in top junior classrooms. If children have to walk too far, perhaps to the school library, to find a suitable book, this alone may inhibit reluctant readers.

6 Children should be encouraged to take school books home, and to bring books and other materials from home into the classroom.

7 Some children are almost totally dependent on the school for suitable reading materials; it is thus vitally important that such pupils do not equate reading simply with the reading scheme.

8 Children should be encouraged to discuss informally why they have chosen a book and what they have thought of their choice.

9 We should not give the impression that reading matter is synonymous with the glossy products of professional writers. Children have as authentic a voice, opinions and ideas as their adult counterparts and their stories, books, poems and plays should mingle with the professional texts in the classroom.

10 Children should be helped to make an informed choice of both fiction and non-fiction materials for themselves. They should not be spoonfed with a prescribed set of pages to read for their topic inquiry, but rather should be taught how to home in on the necessary information, using all the

appropriate study skills and exploiting a contents page, index, chapter headings, illustrations, diagrams, dictionary or other reference work.

11   Books which invite reader participation[21] are deservedly popular with children but as readers they should be encouraged to employ this active questioning whatever the material.

12   Fiction may imprint more indelible images of right and wrong, of cultural, racial and gender stereotypes on the child's mind than more overtly homilectic texts, since the polished structure and gripping narrative make fiction particularly memorable. Thus all teachers need to be particularly vigilant about weeding out reading materials which present one gender or the other, a particular profession or group, a class or race in a limited or distorted way. Simultaneously we need to make every effort to present more positive images of less prestigious groups. These are very obvious first moves but our concern should be to reinforce these through the hidden curriculum. There is little point rejecting books which present girls in purely domestic roles if we then, however subconsciously, appear to discourage boys from cleaning up after art and craft sessions or react quite differently to individuals who give in untidy work or behave roughly in the playground, merely because of their gender. There is little point in choosing books which present racial minorities in a positive manner if we simultaneously give the impression that teachers are inevitably of higher status than cleaners or dinner ladies.

13   All teachers need to bring the ideas and literature of other cultures into the classroom. Arguably, it is the cosily rural or suburban 'white' primary schools which are most in need of reaching out to other cultures. Reaching out may take a variety of forms and those of us who feel inexperienced or underconfident will begin modestly, by extending and enriching those activities we would encourage naturally. Where reading is concerned this may mean choosing books such as *The Julian Stories*[22] which present a natural and positive image of non-white groups. We will check that a promising text is not diminished by condescending or inaccurate illustrations. We will take the

important third step of ensuring that if the story is to be read aloud, it is not read in such a way that white characters are seen to be more normal, fluent or rational than black characters and that our questions to the class do not, however implicitly, suggest that white characters are somehow more interesting than black characters.

14   When choosing folk tales or myths, both deservedly popular in the primary classroom, it is important not to limit our choice to those we have, paradoxically, come to see as mainstream, even our own, whether the Greek myths or Hans Andersen's fairy tales. We need to make a conscious effort to integrate the fascinating and equally valuable tales from less familiar cultures. This may require some help and guidance from the local librarian, parents, language or teachers' centre, or from annotated book lists.[23] In some fortunate classrooms the experts may be in residence, pupils who are familiar with Ashanti, Polish, Vietnamese, Jamaican, Irish, Bengali fables or tales, who can add to our understanding, contribute to our book displays and translate the originals. In the multilingual classroom experience of folk tales, fables and myths is enriched by reference to the authentic language of the original, or by translating the tale into all the languages represented in the classroom.

Strategies for reading development

1   Parents are made to feel at least equal partners with the teacher in reading development. They are encouraged in a non-hectoring manner to commence or continue their support of children's reading beyond school hours.[24]

2   Parents are made aware, in a friendly manner, of the school's and class teacher's reading policy and practices, ideally before the child begins school.

3   Parents are encouraged to contribute to the reading programme by working with the teacher, reading with children, discussing the child's or group's reading or acting as a guide[25] in the classroom.

4   Children introduce and promote their own favourite books, to their partner, group or class.

5 Children adapt a story containing lively dialogue (perhaps their own work) for reading aloud.

6 Children produce taped versions of stories, poems, plays, instructions, questions, jokes.

7 Children produce taped versions of the above and invite the listener to suggest options for development, or to predict what might happen next.

8 Children devise, read and revise their own story (etc.) using a word processor.

9 Children are given opportunities to read their own work or the work of others with or to younger children.

10 Children devise illustrations, or produce a slide sequence, to accompany their own writing.

11 Children are encouraged to look critically at a book's 'fixtures and fittings': the covers, illustrations, print type, contents page, index.

12 Children produce a 'Read all about it' broadsheet or display, highlighting books they have read and enjoyed, and those which they would recommend, giving reasons.

13 Children form their own reviewing panel, based loosely perhaps on television book programmes.

14 Children take on the role of children's television's senior dramatist and select key episodes from a story (etc.) for presentation on screen.

15 Children advertise a favourite book as though it was a new and prestigious product.

16 Children demonstrate their understanding of what they have read by adapting it for improvised performance, or for presentation as a puppet play, musical, dumb show (etc.).

17 Children convey the exciting kernel of their reading material to those who do not know it, through mime, improvised drama, puppet play, series of questions, poster, tableau (etc.).

18 Children devise a better method for arranging or classifying the books in the class library.

19 Children take on the role of librarian and answer typical readers' queries, for example: 'I'm looking for a book on ships – I want to draw a Roman galley,' 'I want to find a book on ghosts for my brother, he's only eight,' 'I want to know how many legs a centipede really has.'

20 The teacher introduces new class reading material by enigmatically displaying real objects associated with the text.

21 The teacher helps to give children the confidence to try books which are apparently a little too difficult for them by reading them aloud (or adapting them for reading aloud) in class time.

22 The teacher ensures that, wherever possible, the under-confident or inexperienced reader understands much of what he is about to read in advance,[26] for example by discussing the title and illustrations, through hearing the teacher or others reading it aloud, or through televised or dramatic interpretation.

23 The teacher brings in and comments on appropriate reading materials which she has enjoyed.

24 The teacher builds links between reading materials and television, radio or theatrical adaptations, anticipating forthcoming dramatizations by displaying related materials in the classroom, and seeking pupils' views of the media interpretations.

25 The teacher enters 'in role' as a character from a work the class is currently interested in and challenges children to deduce who she is from her responses to their questions.

26 The teacher engineers opportunities for bringing 'real life' stories into the classroom, including those recounted through newspaper reports, letters, diaries, biographies and children's anecdotes.

27 The teacher helps pupils to collect books associated with a theme, in part to demonstrate the options that face the author or reader when contemplating any subject.

28 The teacher ensures that every child not only understands the classification system of the classroom and school library, but also has ample opportunities for practising use of both.

29 The teacher encourages the children to select which reading materials are shortlisted for prominence in the class library or book display.

30 The teacher ensures that all pupils are benefiting from reading practice, not merely those fortunate few who habitually complete written work first.

31 The teacher ensures that reading is not happening in

insignificant fits and starts, of the kind described in recent research surveys,[27] but goes to some lengths to guarantee time for 'USSR' (Uninterrupted Sustained Silent Reading).[28]

32 The teacher enables children to make optimum use of USSR time by ensuring that they have an appropriate choice of reading materials and a comfortable niche in which to read, whether on chair, cushion or floor, at a table or in a corner.

33 The teacher encourages each child to develop a positive reading self-image. Rather than stressing failure, she helps each child to build upon successes, finding opportunities for even (especially) the least proficient to shine, not necessarily as readers aloud, but as presenters of materials that they have read and enjoyed.

34 The teacher exploits all the visual aids available, particularly high-quality television programmes, in order to make reading development memorable and fun.

Assessing reading

1 Children do not develop as readers in a crude sequential manner. Their reading abilities are relative, that is context bound, and related to the text before them and to the circumstances in which it is read. If the child is uninterested by the text or inhibited by the surroundings the quality of the reading will suffer. Reading tests are, almost without exception, seriously flawed because they attempt to assess reading progress in a hermetically sealed context which bears little relationship to normal reading.

2 Rather than labelling the reader's mistakes when reading aloud, it is more logical and helpful to think of these as miscues,[29] which reveal the reading strategies which the child is attempting or neglecting. Diagnosis of the successes and problems can then lead to help related to specific difficulties.

3 Exercises which present pupils with short extracts, followed by comprehension questions, do not sensibly test true comprehension, particularly where they are based on unknown material which is inadequately introduced. Such exercises are inevitably artificial. The pupil knows that the

41

questions will inexorably follow; he is thus not reading for pleasure or even for information in the usual sense, but is normally doing so in order to complete a routine task as quickly as possible.

4 Comprehension exercises seldom come close to the reality of normal and natural reading, where the 'active', successful reader will question and reflect as he goes. Pupils would do better to question, discuss and review the reading matter with their colleagues or with the teacher. Ideal comprehension questions are not those posed by a distant writer, but those suggested by the pupil or the group. The aim is not to make children passively dependent on alien comprehension questions which tediously follow course book extracts, but to help them to pose and answer such questions for themselves.

5 The teacher's role is to focus attention in order to help children to evaluate what they have read, for example where characters have faced dilemmas, done wrong, or where pupils' own experiences are related to the text: 'Why do you think James locked the door? Would you have done the same thing if you had been him?' 'Have you ever had to take a risk to help someone?'

6 Comprehension can be tested painlessly and creatively in a number of ways, since comprehension can result in a wide range of finished products, not merely the stilted, largely copied comprehension answer. Thus, children may read instructions in order to make a model, decide roles, follow a route, play a game or cook a dish. Ideally pupils should devise instructions for themselves, with a target audience in mind, and should evaluate the quality of these instructions in practice.

7 Children may choose to convey their understanding of a story, poem, scenario, report, letter or diagram through drama, art or craft work or through imaginative and factual writing.

8 Children are likely to make little effort to comprehend factual reading matter, typically for topic work, if they face situations which seem to invite passive copying and which sidestep the study skills which are so important in any kind of research.

9 The acquisition of study skills cannot be left to chance.

Children need to be taught how to exploit libraries and reference works. Their grasp of these skills should be assessed through meaningful tasks.

10 If we envisage the way real researchers work we are less likely to invite arbitrary, artificial or irrelevant topic tasks. The most meaningful assignments are likely to be pupil-motivated. The child stumbles upon a problem, perhaps she wants to give an authentically Australian background to her story about sharks but has never visited the country; she seeks out the information for her own purposes and thus the need fuels the research.

11 It is never too early to ask children to evaluate the truth of what they have read. While we should not encourage a depressing cynicism, active questioning is healthy. Occasionally, it is legitimate to jolt pupils' critical faculties with material which contains flaws in logic or which includes significant omissions. Outdated reference works, sadly plentiful in school libraries which have been frozen in their 1970s' state by later capitation cuts, can be used to demonstrate how vigilant readers must be to look at the date when a book was written, by whom and for what purpose. Older children, at least, can plan and produce debates which show that there are always at least two sides to every question, and can compare several newspaper reports which purport to describe the same event.

12 Some teachers may wish to jolt older pupils' susceptibilities by demonstrating the dangerous power of authority figures, including the teacher, not by foolishly faking the aftermath of a nuclear attack as one primary school head teacher did recently, but by introducing nonsensical but non-racial and non-religious opinions in a rational manner. This must be done discreetly, in a controlled and supportive context since pupils may be angry to find their trust abused. The teacher may demonstrate or invite pupils to convince their colleagues that the earth really is flat after all or that our ancestors had a primeval third leg. If the exercise is to be worthwhile, the readers or listeners should be encouraged to identify and demolish the meretriciously persuasive tactics which have been used.

Alternatives to the conventional reading scheme

In recent years an increasing number of educational writers and practitioners have questioned the rationale and practical value of the conventional sequential reading scheme. They have suggested that the reading scheme is not merely outmoded but that it actively distorts and contradicts some of the learning theories and teaching strategies which are apparently held most dear in primary education: the notion of child-centred rather than curriculum-centred education; the desirability of integration of subject areas wherever possible, rather than arbitrary fragmentation; the importance of helping the child to develop on a broad front at his own pace, rather than an insistence on the sequential acquisition of skills. The conventional reading scheme, in its approach to reading as a discrete skill and in its emphasis on the graded reader which must be mastered before a more difficult book can be attempted, does undoubtedly undermine all these principles.

This growing scepticism about the value and purpose of the reading scheme is nothing new; glimmers of it can be detected in the *Plowden Report*:

> Among the most welcome changes which have accompanied
> the growing informality of the primary school has been the
> move away from categories of books, each confined to a
> special time and purpose. In many schools there are no
> longer class readers, supplementary readers, group readers,
> text books and library books. . . . There are simply books –
> to be used as and when they are needed.[30]

The *Bullock Report* was based 'on the important principle that reading must be seen as part of a child's general language development and not as a discrete skill which can be considered in isolation from it'.[31] Regarding the use of reading schemes, the committee commented:

> We are certainly not advocating that the school should
> necessarily use one, and we welcome the enterprise of those
> schools which have successfully planned the teaching of
> reading without the use of a graded series.[32]

A number of educational initiatives in the past twenty years have sought to provide alternatives to the graded reading scheme, based upon a more global 'language experience' approach to the teaching of reading.

The language experience approach

'Breakthrough to Literacy'

The 'Breakthrough to Literacy' materials, first published in 1969, and emanating from the Schools Council 'Programme in Linguistics and English Teaching', build upon an understanding of early language development and upon the belief that learning to read and write, far from being separate English activities, are firmly embedded in language development as a whole. When using the programme, children are significantly encouraged to generate their own written materials as early as possible, thus 'learning language, and learning through language'.[33] Children begin, not with an introductory reader, but with a personal Sentence Maker consisting of words commonly used by children, printed on cards, which are supplemented by the children's own requested words, usually supplied by the teacher.

Instead of beginning by reading the materials of others, children integrate the writing and reading of their own materials. With the help of the Sentence Maker they can arrange words to say what they want before they have the manual dexterity necessary to write. Such a process means that children are first meeting reading materials which reflect their own expectations of colloquial language, thus making reading prediction easier. Children are usually introduced to the Breakthrough format through the teacher's use of her own enlarged Sentence Maker. They are given their own Sentence Maker after they can recognize perhaps eight to fifteen printed words. The essential Sentence Maker is supplemented, when appropriate, by the Project Folder (a blank version of the Sentence Maker), by My First Word Book (a first dictionary) and by the First and Second Word Makers (containing vowels, consonants and blends which encourage children to try out the spellings of new words). The Breakthrough books are designed to be read to the children and discussed with them before being read by the children themselves, something which occurs only after they have done a substantial amount of composing with their own Sentence Makers.

Given that the Breakthrough materials are built upon enlightened learning principles – the notion of building upon children's existing knowledge of and interest in language; recognition of the importance of encouraging children to generate language, rather than merely decoding and responding to the writing of others – it is perhaps surprising that the programme is not more popular in primary schools. HMI reported in 1978 that it was only being used in 7 per cent of the infant schools they surveyed and found overwhelming evidence of the popularity of more traditional reading schemes in infant classrooms.[34]

'Ginn Reading 360'

The Ginn 360 programme offers an 'all-round approach . . . to reading and language learning'[35] for pre-readers through to those with a reading age of 13, via an integrated course in comprehension, language and study skills. The materials for Level One embrace six Readers, a Wordbank (consisting of word cards and character cards, derived from the Readers), Magic Circle 'extension' books, Activity Books and a Listening Skills and Language Development Pack of tapes and discussion pictures. By Level Nine, intended broadly for 8- to 9-year-olds, the Readers provide the core of the programme, supplemented by comprehension cards and duplicating masters.

The Ginn 360 programme does commendably build upon the *Bullock Report*'s[36] recommendation that the teaching of reading should continue throughout the junior years and beyond, and it goes to some lengths to avoid the worst excesses of earlier readers of the 'Up Spot, up. Jump up, up, says John' variety. But although the Ginn scheme claims, justifiably, to be a 'multi-method' approach where reading is developed through reading, writing, speaking and listening, it is not a radical departure from the conventional reading scheme. Readers are at the heart of the scheme, not at the edges as in the Breakthrough to Literacy materials. Unlike Breakthrough, which devolves much of the responsibility for the selection and manipulation of language to the child, the Ginn programme places the teacher, or rather the authors, firmly in control, introducing new words in an orderly sequence and tying the related activities quite tightly to these new words. Beyond Level Eight the emphasis is increasingly on comprehension exercises which, under the direction of the less competent and enlightened teacher, could come to dominate the reading curriculum in an artificial and pedestrian way, particularly where children are asked to read a story and fill in the answers without adequate preliminary and subsequent discussion.

Given the cost of the entire Ginn 360 package, and the amount of classroom time required if a fair range of associated activities is to be attempted, it is easy to see how a 'lowest common denominator' approach may evolve, based at its worst in the junior years on reading aloud to teacher accompanied by single and silent concentration on the relevant comprehension exercise. Of course no learning programme is entirely teacher-proof and in the hands of the enlightened the Ginn programme can work well. It has been welcomed by many teachers who have, rightly, become disillusioned with the earlier more limited schemes, including some who have abandoned Ladybird readers. They have introduced it as an 'all through' scheme which modestly places reading in a wider language context, while still retaining the security of structured readers.

Real books for real readers

Many teachers believe that the reading scheme, whether used singly or, more often, integrated with at least one other scheme, offers the only way of guaranteeing systematic reading progress, of helping to ensure that children meet reading materials at the right level at the right time. Some, more cynically, would suggest that the dominance of reading schemes owes as much to inertia as to any coherent rationale; they are there, they were expensively acquired, we have to use them, particularly where there is no apparent affordable alternative.

The authors of the *Extending Beginning Reading* report disclosed some of the worst results of an uncritical and unmonitored reliance on the reading scheme:

47

(i) A second-year child of below average reading ability spent over 6 months reading Wide Range Book 4;

(ii) A second-year child of above average reading ability spent 6 months reading Wide Range Book 5.[37]

They conclude by asking:

> Is there any good reason for relying so heavily on the reading schemes currently available, with their disjointed collections of short stories and other items? Might it not be better to grade the majority of all the books in the school, as simply and speedily as possible, and then allow children to select their own books, at particular levels, according to their own interests?[38]

An increasing number of teachers would enthusiastically reply 'Yes' to these questions. They are the teachers who have been led to rethink their approaches to the teaching of reading, by the recognition of poor materials, poor results, the advent of a new head teacher or language postholder, or by the sudden dawning of the obvious, that there are viable alternatives. They would agree wholeheartedly with Jill Bennett that:

> reading is not about look and say, word-by-word decoding, phonic analysis or a progression through boring reading schemes. It is, first of all, a matter of getting meaning from print. . . . The ability to read is developed through reading and this implies allowing and encouraging beginners to behave like readers.[39]

Encouraging children to behave like real readers will generally mean trusting them to choose their own reading materials, allowing them the time to read at length for pleasure, and encouraging children to show initiative and independence in the selection and execution of classroom activities, thus freeing time for the teacher to read *at length* and uninterrupted *with* individuals.

The experiences of a group of London teachers, who chose the 'real books' alternative, suggest what this may mean in practice:

It was felt that the books we had on offer were increasingly out of date and out of place, reflecting neither the background of the children, nor the philosophy of the school. Some did not even tell a good story. We decided the books on offer in a reading programme should be of literary worth, should convey a good tale, and should stimulate a response to meaning. In short the books should engage the child's interest and encourage further reading.[40]

These teachers bought a large selection of picture books with interest throughout the primary age range, books for early readers and fiction which would stretch the most proficient. They also ordered multiple copies of many books, in order to encourage the sharing and discussion of texts:

Joining a group of upper juniors communally reading Peter Dickinson's 'Heartsease' tells us so much about each child's progress, not just in the area of reading words on a page, but also about his/her overall view as to how he/she is seeing the fictional world operate. An observing teacher overheard a child who reads aloud haltingly, lead a discussion on the intentions and actions of the main characters with a fine understanding of human nature.

Such innovations significantly built upon existing successful reading practices, thus 'Story Time' was used to introduce new books and these books were in turn part read and part improvised by groups of young readers. The sharing and discussion of texts led to greater sharing and discussion of the children's written work which was increasingly seen as the work of real authors.

Liz Waterland, deputy head teacher in a Peterborough infants school, has described[41] at greater length the implications of a real books policy. She rejects the behaviourist model, which sees the reader as operated on by the demands of the text, in favour of an apprenticeship model which sees the reader as operating on the text, contributing as much to the material as this does to the reader. She suggests that the teacher's role is to provide a wide range of real books from which the child will choose those which are meaningful to him:

The adult first reads all the story while the child cannot read any, then the child will put in the words she or he knows while the adult reads the rest, then the child will take over the reading. All this with a known text first of all, rather as the child learnt to speak a little at a time in forms that were familiar, until finally enough vocabulary is acquired to tackle new text (although still with an adult to help if needed).[42]

This process of successive approximation can only work, she suggests, where the child knows where the story is going before he attempts to read it, and where failure and competition are removed from the reading process. More so than Ginn 360, more even than Breakthrough, this apprenticeship approach stresses the vitally important work of parents in reinforcing and supporting these methods at home. Thus, young readers take their chosen books home in a 'book bag' and parents are asked to read the story with the child, just as the teacher would in the classroom, ensuring that the child can see the print and pictures, pointing to the words as they are read, exploiting the illustrations and allowing ample time for discussion of the 'What do you think will happen next?' type. Such activities can then lead gradually to the child choosing to read the same story himself in a supportive situation in which all attempts are praised. Significantly, as with the earlier London example, these reading methods are combined with an approach to writing which encourages children to produce their own books, thus demonstrating the structure of written language and giving the child power over its manipulation.

Such apparently laissez-faire approaches to reading cause some to ask, 'But how do you assess progress?' Liz Waterland counters convincingly in two ways, by suggesting that record sheets, checklists and the like tell us little about the strategies, understanding and enjoyment the child is bringing to the book, and by suggesting a sequence of reading behaviours which are related not to reading age or experience but to the particular text the child is encountering. Thus, with undeniable logic and common sense, she suggests that 'any one child may show several different kinds of behaviour depending on what is being read, or even several different kinds of behaviour within one book'. She pinpoints what many sensitive parents know only too well: 'There may be three or four different reading behaviours and levels of response within one ten-minute period with one text.'[43]

Conclusion

Given that almost all primary age children learn to read, in a perfunctory sense at least, whatever method is used, and given the understandable apathy which many children display, however quietly, when they are asked to take out their reader, or read to the teacher, it makes sense to choose classroom reading approaches which interest the child and which:

1 Conform most closely to real reading.
2 Logically dovetail with the best preschool and beyond school reading practices employed by parents.
3 Demonstrate that reading is worthwhile and stimulating, since if we are not reading fiction for pleasure, what else is the rationale?
4 Coincide with children's own (indeed adults' own) notions of pleasurable reading.
5 Encourage the kind of initiative, in the selection and use of books, which we would hope to develop throughout the curriculum, throughout the school.
6 Remove much of the stress, competition and testing which too often bedevil learning to read.
7 Do not, without good reason, restrict the child's choice of books.
8 Acknowledge that learning to read is not a linear, nor a once and for all process, but one which involves concurrent, pleasurable encounters with many kinds of materials, for many kinds of purposes.

3

Writing: processes and purposes

The nature of writing

It is not an exaggeration to claim that for almost all of us, writing is a rather artificial and minor medium for communication. With very few exceptions, we communicate through the spoken word, only resorting to writing when oral communication is impossible. Once we have, usually laboriously, learned how to write, even those of us employed in educational institutions exploit only a narrow range of writing purposes: writing a cheque, a formal and occasionally informal letter, a shopping list, a memo, completing a form. The writing is usually perfunctory, seldom extended, rarely imaginative and overwhelmingly utilitarian. Those who write imaginative prose or poetry for the love of it are sometimes seen as slightly eccentric creatures; those who produce such works for publication are set apart as 'writers' and 'poets', with all the nineteenth century connotations that these epithets inevitably trail.

Children learn to talk long before they learn to write, and the 'learning' to talk is quite distinct from the school learning which is generally associated with early attempts at writing. The motivation to speak is enormous; the young child does not need to be informed of the importance of the spoken word since he has ample proof of what it can achieve through witnessing the many ways in which language is generated and used in the home: to build relationships, express identity, emotion, desires, to discover, persuade, negotiate, entertain, plan, describe, to make sense of a bewildering world, and as a medium which can be used for sheer fun, in order to relish words. There are no lessons, no rules, no punishments, no objectives, no competition, no formal assessment, indeed none of the normal accompaniments to school learning. The feedback, particularly from loving parents, is immediate and usually approving. It picks up on the child's utterances and extends and elaborates them, providing the child with yet more models. Through a process of imitation, experimentation and generalization from these models, the child's use of language approximates more and more closely to the norms of adult utterance and simultaneously broadens as he comes to understand the registers of language use, distinguishing the tones, vocabulary and syntax appropriate to informal play with a friend from that reserved for more intimidating formal encounters with adult authority figures. Some of this learning will come closer to school learning: 'Don't talk to your Grandad like that,' 'We don't call it that in our gang,' but much of it will be invisible, even apparently innate, since some children are astute in feeling the temperature for appropriate language use, given the nature of the context and the audience. The child will home in on the models provided by friends, family, and not least television.

Learning to talk is a generally painless process which happens within a supportive environment, before the child begins school. By the time he joins the reception class he is well aware of the importance of talk and of many of the purposes to which it can be put. But for most children learning to write happens outside the home, in an artificial and very bewildering environment called a school, and for apparently no good reason. For many learning to write will appear to be an arbitrary business, for a few it may seem to be a sadistically devised process. The child will probably have witnessed few instances of his parents writing anything which had an obvious rationale to the child and he is most unlikely to have seen his parents writing fiction or poetry. If writing has any sort of importance, it will have acquired this almost incidentally through reading, when the child wishes to generate the kind of literature that he or his parents have enjoyed reading. But even learning to read, difficult though it is for many, has a distinct advantage over learning to write. Reading works from the unknown to the known unlocking a code which should give immediate and satisfying feedback, particularly where the child is reconstructing at will a much loved story which, until then, he has had to beg an adult to read to him. Writing is a slow process, annoyingly involving hands, surfaces and materials which complicate the whole affair. It works from the known sound to the unknown symbols, a most disconcerting direction, since where in reading the context will be helpful in signalling obvious possibilities and mistakes, in writing the written symbols can look comfortingly correct when they express gibberish. This discrepancy is seen at its most obvious when the writer of nonsense remembers and 'reads' what he hoped to say, quite oblivious of these mistakes. We can compare this essential difference between reading and writing with the analogy of translating from and into a foreign language. Most find it easier to translate from the written foreign form (from the unknown to the known) than to translate into a foreign language (from the known into the unknown), since in the latter case the options are so unnervingly wide. Thus, at the greater conceptual level learning to write demands a considerable act of faith from the child, since he is unlikely to understand how writing can help him, and at the local cognitive level writing is a frightening stab in the dark since the gulf between familiar sound and apparently arbitrary phoneme is so great.

For the child who is unaware of any good reason for writing, the next conundrums to be answered are how to write and what to write, and particularly how to sustain writing. Where talking seems to come naturally, in the sense that the child will be quite unaware of the working of his vocal cords, jaws and lungs, writing includes 'foreign bodies' which form barriers between the thought in the head and the product on the page. Overt physiological processes are involved, the manipulation of the pencil and paper, and the positioning of the body. Children soon learn that while they are drawing abstract squiggles they are safe but once they move into the adult world of real letters, the problems begin to proliferate since mistakes can be challenged and the possibilities for mistakes are manifold: incorrect sizes and shapes, words run together, illegibility, incorrect positioning on the page or direction of letters and the omission of words or letters. And there is no precedent for this minefield since talk appears invisible, unchallengeable at the handwriting and spelling levels.

The problems however extend beyond the surface features of written language, since accuracy, fraught though it is, is not enough. The teacher is also interested in what you have written; content counts and here the problems are altogether different and more intransigent because they are more nebulous. At least with accuracy there is a right and wrong; the teacher will be consistent, will insist that bicycle is always spelt thus, that the stem of a 'd' is always higher than that on an 'a', but the rules for successful content are more difficult to grasp and for many children can only be incidentally inferred, should they be motivated to do so, from the teacher's enigmatic comments once the writing has been completed: 'A good story Hywel,' 'I liked the ending Lisa.' This kind of assessment is altogether different from that provided by the listener and participant during a conversation.

It is difficult to tie down the precise nature of writing, in part because it involves so much and because the product is merely the tip of a vast invisible iceberg. The tip displays the result for perusal and the transcription skills of handwriting, spelling and punctuation, but alone seldom tells us anything about the composition process which has led to this. Composition encapsulates many processes, planning, reviewing, anticipating, rewriting and editing. Just because composition is so often, and particularly in classrooms, such a private and solitary activity, it is difficult to expose its processes to the light of day, in the way we might with the building of polysyllabic words or the taking apart of a model to see how it works. Teachers thus have difficulty teaching composition and, more significantly, children will tend to lack successful models for their own composition. This is manifested in the far from extreme 'light blue touch paper' school of creative writing, where a routine and apparently random stimulus is introduced by the teacher, perhaps a bald title or an artifact, and children are expected to 'get on with it' with little or no chance to make these subjects their own through careful thought, discussion or questioning. Of course those children who have already mastered the art of giving the teacher what she appears to want will have few problems and the fact that they do well may dangerously legitimize this practice in the teacher's eyes, implying that if a minority can succeed it is the fault of the majority if they fail to glean what is expected. It is little wonder if many children's conception of 'writing' diverges markedly from the teacher's own aims for writing. While we may see this as an important umbrella term, denoting much that is educationally valuable in the classroom, some children will confuse it with the narrow transcription skill of handwriting, while others will see it as synonymous with work: 'Get on with your work Peter,' or with control: 'Since I can't trust you to keep the noise down you'll have to go back to writing.'

Why write?

Given the importance of oral communication, the often onerous nature of writing, and technological advances which increasingly obviate the need to write anything at length and particularly in longhand, we may question why we need ask our pupils to write anything at all. Of course we might also inquire 'Why read?' 'Why talk?' 'Why poetry?' 'Why drama?' but with writing the need to answer this question honestly is more pressing, since so much classroom time is devoted to writing and because it is accorded so much prestige. Talk is still seen unfortunately as an ephemeral upstart, while writing has the official imprimatur of literature and the examination system, and not least society's expectations of what education is all about. These intangible but nevertheless pervasive and powerful factors may lead us to assume that writing is *per se* a good thing and that to give children a lot of it is at best highly beneficial, and at worst harmless reinforcement. The Assessment of Performance Unit's survey of the language performance of 11-year-old pupils suggests how many children may actively dislike writing in school. At least one in five of those in their sample stated that they did not value writing as a source of personal satisfaction and that they tried to write as little as possible, and one in four of the sample felt that they were asked to write too much at school and anticipated that they would not write much when they left school. A third of those surveyed indicated that 'they couldn't see the point of their written work'.[1]

Such disconcerting findings have been confirmed by those disclosed through the School Curriculum Development Committee's 'National Writing Project': 'Children see "writing" as an activity which simply provides teachers with something to correct. This attitude is reinforced as they listen to teachers, parents and politicians who seem to think all that matters is that writing is spelled correctly and set out neatly – important considerations indeed but not the *most* important.'[2]

What, then, is the rationale for asking children to produce the particular kind of imaginative, fictional writing which so characterizes the teaching of English in primary schools? There are several possible answers:

Practising this kind of imaginative writing may:

1 Help children to acquire those creative writing skills which will be valuable in later life.
2 Help children to acquire the necessary transcription skills, spelling, punctuation and handwriting.
3 Keep children engrossed and quiet.
4 Help to initiate and develop relationships with others through, for example, pair and group writing and the production of written instructions, directions, stories, letters, plays and poems which have target audiences in mind, or may invite direct responses.
5 Produce artefacts which satisfy the writer and edify and entertain readers.
6 Help to crystallize the writer's own feelings and opinions, sometimes therapeutically, often as the basis for further consideration.
7 Encourage the kind of empathic identification, perhaps through writing 'in role', which may, in certain circumstances, lead to a greater understanding of another's circumstances and reactions.
8 Provide a record or plan, which has implications for future action or work.
9 Encourage children to enjoy the process of writing, irrespective of the quality of the final product.

Taking these propositions in turn, the available evidence suggests that the first, unfortunately, claims too much. While creative writing skills will be valuable in later life, they are unlikely to be valued by society, and there is little evidence to suggest that the writing undertaken in schools provides children with the incentive to continue with imaginative writing beyond school hours or their school career. The second proposition is also over-optimistic. Writing of the routine kind which is too often invited in classrooms does not in itself teach the transcription skills (just as reading does not teach spelling). However, the child's wish to see a satisfying piece of writing presented as correctly as possible may inspire an attention to the details of spelling, punctuation and handwriting.

The third proposition hints at the uncomfortable truth that for many of us writing is, however implicitly, a form of social control. We 'divide and conquer' when we split up a boisterous discussion group and ask them to present their findings separately, in writing. We use writing sessions as oases in which to gather our wits or find time to see individuals or organize resources. These practices, for good and ill, are part of the fabric of teaching methodology and classroom organization. There is nothing wrong with exploiting writing sensitivity to focus the child's attention or to encourage deliberation, but we must be prepared to ask ourselves, 'Why are they writing now?' 'Will this particular activity help me to meet my objectives for them?' 'Does the child have sufficient "investment" in the writing to make it a worthwhile and enjoyable activity?' 'Have I subjugated writing to a crude device for meeting philosophically unsound objectives?'

Writing can, as the fourth proposition suggests, escape from the stereotype of the lone and introverted writer agonizing before entrusting words to paper, to flourish as a healthily collaborative activity where ideas are bounced off colleague or group, or where individuals accept responsibility for certain parts of the writing. The permutations are multiplied once we add the range of possible relationships with audiences: the group trying to devise a fail-safe algorithm which will help their peers, the younger pupils who may laugh at their witty sketch, the parents who may answer their questions.

The remaining propositions together define a legitimate rationale for a wide range of imaginative writing and, while these aims will be achieved to different extents, depending on the maturity and motivation of the writers, infant and junior age children can, in suitable circumstances, meet them all. It would be heartening to know that children understood that these last five propositions contributed to the rationale for imaginative writing; unfortunately it is apparent that many have a very narrow or confused impression of the reasons why we invite them to write imaginatively. A recent, albeit small-scale analysis of 10- and 11-year-old pupils' conceptions of writing[3] revealed that 'Very few children believed that imagination could be concerned with plausible everyday events and the feelings of the participants in those events; and even fewer children understood imagination as a process in which aspects of one's own first-hand experiences were reconstructed'.[4] The authors conclude,

> The first essential, then, is that teachers should clearly understand the functions and characteristics of various kinds of writing, and the second essential is that these are made quite explicit to their pupils. By doing this children can be made sensitive to the various criteria governing good writing in all its forms, and thus be helped to place greater emphasis on qualitative aspects of writing in contrast to mechanical skills.[5]

Such moves may go some way towards helping the child who is largely unaware of what writing can achieve, has little personal motivation for indulging in it, and has no notion of the criteria for success.

Models for writing

Children of primary school age tend to equate imaginative writing with the ubiquitous 'story'. It is not difficult to see why this should be so; the great majority of the imaginative writing which is produced in primary classrooms falls into the story category, a reflection of pupil predilection, the models provided through reading, and of the belief of many teachers that this is the genre of imaginative writing which is most accessible to children. Clearly, first person narratives, however slight, constitute a more natural part of conversation than poetry, and first person autobiographical tales are actively invited by parents, teachers and friends: 'Tell Granny what we did at the zoo. . . ,' 'Who'd like to tell us about their summer holidays?' Children, like adults, become accustomed to story telling on their feet, using the chronological past tense and cementing the narrative with 'ands' and 'thens', in part because these simplify the task and in part because of their familiarity. It is little wonder that when younger children, in particular, are invited to write a story, though it may begin quite objectively in the third person, it may soon home in on the writer's own experiences, sometimes abandoning the third person altogether, in favour of the more familiar 'I'. Many children come to assimilate the conventions of the traditional tale, the use of the past tense, of repetition and of familiar beginnings and endings: 'Once upon a time there was. . . ,' 'And he woke up and it was all a dream,' 'And they lived happily ever after.'

The danger is that unless the teacher intervenes to suggest other models, young writers will take the apparent line of least resistance, producing a story even when a free choice is given. They may assume that since this has pleased her in the past and seems to be what other pupils are producing, it is the only safe choice. It is as easy for the teacher to give pseudo choices as it is to pose pseudo open questions, where, for example, we helpfully suggest 'It doesn't have to be a story' but fail to indicate feasible alternatives and appear to penalize children who choose poetic or play forms by assessing their work more stringently than the rest. It is easy too to underestimate the force of peer group pressure. 'High status' pupils can popularize a less usual approach by adopting it successfully; conversely, where they abandon an approach disillusioned, other less confident children may assume that their aspirations will be similarly blighted.

There is no principle in developmental psychology which would bar children, of whatever age, from writing in play form or verse. Play form manifestations are familiar to most children from television, even if the script on the page is less so, and verse forms erupt in the playground, in advertising and in nursery rhymes. There is no reason why children should not experiment for fun with a variety of written forms so long as the less able or confident are not left with the impression that there are certain forms that are denied to them. We should avoid assumptions of the kind: Wayne will never be able to finish that so he had better not start. Wayne may not be able to write a full-length novel or a five-act play, few adults could successfully, but if he chooses to have a go at writing at length over an extended period of time then he should not be stopped at the outset. Wayne and others will only wish to be this ambitious if such possibilities are opened to them and if the taking of risks is seen as exciting rather than as dangerous and presumptuous.

Although divisive, it is convenient to think of forms of writing in terms of prose, poetry and drama. Thus, at some stage in their primary careers, children might choose to read and write examples of the following:

Prose: letter, story, diary, summary (though only where there is a good reason for doing so), report, autobiography, biography, advertisement, invitation, list, recipe, etc.
Poetry: 'free' verse, shape poetry, haiku, limerick, doggerel, ballad, jingle, song lyric, rhyming couplets, even conceivably ode, sonnet, epic, etc.
Drama: monologue, dialogue, melodrama, farce, revue, etc.

We might add to these types the tones or approaches which add a distinctive dimension to any piece of writing: recording, describing, persuading, inviting, imagining, satirizing, eulogizing, criticizing; comedy, tragedy, burlesque, science fiction, romance; the detective story, fairy story, western, ghost story, horror story. . . . The range is enormous, and has its dangers since these are emphatically not hoops to be jumped through in a defined sequence. Ideally children will choose to read or write or hear examples of the above; such choices are made more likely where children have access to some at least of these kinds of literature. Thus, the teacher may diverge from story reading in order to include letters or diary entries, an 'authentic' document may spring from some drama work, and a group may collaborate to produce an advertising jingle suitable for commercial radio. Once they are made aware of possible forms and approaches, most children jump at them, proving in many cases to be more inventive than their teachers. Thus children may not have met an example of a rhyming shopping list or recipe but may feel that it would be fun and appropriate to try their hands at these variations in which transactional intention and poetic mode can collide effectively, as happens in comic satire where, for example, a politician's literary pretensions are mocked.

While some attempt has been made to account for the understandable supremacy of story writing in many classrooms, we should not underestimate the complex demands made of the writer of stories. To read, tell, or listen to a story is one thing, to write one is quite a different matter, since the short story is a

61

distinct literary genre, demanding at the very least Aristotle's beginning, middle and end, and constraining the writer to provide the required information in an economical yet memorable manner. Even where the story is heavily auto-biographical, and this at least closes down some of the plot options, it has to be shaped and has to meet the reader's need for scene-setting information, information which may seem redundant to the younger and more egocentric writer since he knows he knows it all already.

We should not assume that writing a story, even writing a diary, is necessarily going to be easier for the writer than producing a poem or a piece of dialogue. This is particularly true when the teacher's thirst for stories or diary entries appears unquenchable. We may think that we are doing our pupils a favour by asking them to fill in diaries or journals, describing what they did during the holidays or over the weekend, but these are more onerous tasks than they at first seem. The argument runs: this is the kind of expressive writing, closest to anecdotal and colloquial speech, which should come most readily to children. After all they have merely to tell the truth and describe what happened. It appears however that many children are bored by the diary routine, and some fear and resent it, even going to the lengths of begging parents to take them somewhere, 'So I've got something to write about on Monday.' It is a bewildering task to sum up a whole weekend, let alone a whole holiday. There is a tendency, even among adults, for the mind to flit magpie-like back and forth, rejecting, sifting, camouflaging 'the truth' because it is considered too painful, too boring, or just not suitable for the teacher's perusal. In short, writing should never get into a rut and we should dispassionately gauge the likely results of repeated demands that children produce a narrow range of personal writing. Pupils who choose to keep journals can be encouraged in their course but no child should be forced to divulge his private life unless he wishes to do so.

The classroom climate

We will not come close to helping children to make sense of, and have fun with, this abstract, arcane and complex process called writing unless we make the empathic leap to see this process, as far as possible, from each child's point of view. The truth is that it takes a writer to know how difficult it can be to write, particularly to write to order in an often less than ideal environment. It is also true that primary teachers have little overt incentive to write imaginatively. It is never required of them by their superiors, and is rarely demanded by the curriculum. Literature, for many teachers, is something produced by others, whether the professional writer or the pupils. There are so many excellent story books and poetry anthologies on the market that we may feel inhibited by the thought of attempting to emulate them. Instead, teachers' writing time is filled with perfunctory form filling and report writing; professionally produced project materials and the advent of the 'all in' language and reading scheme may even tend to squeeze out teachers' own curriculum products, even at the workcard level. And yet, only by writing our own poetry, prose or scripts will we know how unnerving the blank sheet, the deadline (or lack of it), the fixed option or plethora of choices can be. To write is to remind oneself, as I am reminded now, of the many immediate and potential distractions from the task. There are those that come uninvited, the backfiring car, the intrusive questioner; there are those which we choose for ourselves, in a desperate attempt to forestall the awful moment of starting a new book, chapter, or even page or sentence. There are the rewards and releases we promise ourselves for doing just one more page, the cup of tea, the walk around the room, the switching on of the radio. There are the devices which many use to sustain the flow of precious words, to prevent the horror of the mental block, particularly after an interval; writers like Somerset Maugham who candidly admitted that he dared not stop at the end of a page at the end of the day, but made himself encroach on the whiteness of the next page. It is little wonder that professional writers sometimes appear slightly eccentric and superstitious creatures – Muriel Spark who insists on specially purchased exercise books and pens, some who take the equivalent of the new ball in cricket when they earn the right to move from longhand first draft into typed final draft, and yet more who only work certain hours on certain days. Some will welcome the commissioned work, the fixed length and the deadline, which reduce the deliberation over options for organization and subject matter; others will prefer the scope of a free choice.

Unless the writer is, most unusually, writing only for herself or for undefined heirs, she will have in mind a notional audience, and this may be the most significant factor in deciding what is written and how. The audience will decide such fundamental factors as: the nature and organization of the content; the style, including the choice of vocabulary; the selection of illustrations, where appropriate; the type and size of print. There is a great and disconcerting gulf however between envisaging an audience, knowing in general terms what we are to write about, and finding the right route for saying it. Frank Smith[6] has described this gulf vividly:

> At a global level we know and can specify very well what we want to write about; and at a focal level we have no trouble putting one word after another – provided we can decide what we specifically want to say. But we are lost at the intermediate level – for example, in deciding the exact direction in which we want a paragraph to go. The situation is similar to the common one of knowing our way around a few streets in a neighbourhood of a town we are visiting (a focal level) and understanding very well the relation of the town to the country as a whole (the global level) but having no idea about the relationship of the neighbourhood to the town itself (an intermediate level).[7]

Sometimes these intermediate problems begin to dissolve once the words have been committed to paper; sometimes they can be resolved through periods of thought between writing or after an interval of doing something quite different. Unfortunately pre-writing problems are seldom solved through reference to a colleague since he or she is usually only in a sensible position to judge once the proposed solution can be inspected on paper.

Pupils seldom have even the relative freedom of the adult writer of fiction; the 1978 survey of primary schools indicated that 'Children were frequently involved in writing tasks which had been set by teachers ... much less writing arose from pupils' own choice than is sometimes supposed'.[8] Many pupils are in the peculiar position of writing effectively for a single audience, the teacher. A year of doing this may be comforting since, by the end, the child may be much closer to knowing the criteria for success, but such a concentrated focus on a single reader can result in uncreative complacency, where children have assimilated very narrow (perhaps mistaken) notions of what will please the teacher. Those children, the great majority, who strive to win the teacher's approval are often astute at picking up the signals:

Jeanette: Well, it's mostly fairy tales I write about because Mr A— always commented I've got a good imagination for fairy tales, so I'm about pixies and fairies and goblins and things.[9]

Writing for pleasure demands a classroom climate in which choices and alternatives are continually opening up, where ideas are bounced from child to child, child to teacher and teacher to child, where 'What if . . .?' and 'We thought we'd . . .' are commonly heard. It cannot flourish in a climate of course book assignments where children know that to read a story, poem or extract is to meet the accompanying writing assignment. If adults knew that a written task would inevitably follow much of what they read, reading would be, at best, avoided and, at worst, feared.

Writing, like all meaningful learning activities where large numbers of individuals are involved, requires a climate of controlled freedom. This apparent paradox is reconciled in those classrooms where the freedom to say 'I'd like to . . .' is tempered by a consideration of the needs of others. Children, particularly the less confident, will not express novel, bright and thus potentially risky ideas if they feel that the teacher has allowed an atmosphere to develop in which others, perhaps more able or confident, are likely to snigger or criticize destructively. Children need to acquire gradually the subtle discretion which registers when it is appropriate to intrude into another's 'writing space' or silence and when a well-meaning comment may be seen as tactless. None of this will of course be learned in classrooms where the teacher is herself fragmenting pupil thought, cluttering mental space with her comments, giving layer upon layer of instructions, or discouraging deliberation and meditation by penalizing those who seem miles away. Few will be insensitive enough to snap 'Get on with your work' when a child is staring into space, head in hand, pencil poised, but the interruption can be no less annoying and equally counterproductive when the teacher inquires, 'Everything all right Rachel?'

We need to balance the novelty of new approaches and ideas with the security and routine of expectations that are understood by all in the classroom. Paradoxically, control is necessary if children are to be free to think, and yet there must be room for the sudden change of plan, the sudden burst into speech, drama or indeed any other area of learning. The noise of pre-writing discussion, the quietness of composition and the collaborative whispers which may accompany editing and redrafting are all important. We all benefit from the security of knowing the behavioural expectations for any activity, but these expectations are all the more meaningful where they have been negotiated, and infants are as capable of seeing the reasons for silence, or legitimized noise, as juniors are. The question of the arrangement of the furniture, the positioning and distribution of writing resources, should be shared with the class: here is the question or problem, what is the best solution, given our needs? And what if the majority suggests a solution which the teacher does not favour? So long as it is not patently ridiculous, it can be given a fair trial and then evaluated. Such trials and errors will go some way towards convincing children that they are not squatters in what is essentially the teacher's classroom, there on sufferance as annoying impedimenta, but that they have some investment in the space as well as in the activities that take place there. Such a philosophy may have messy implications; if children are free to write about anything they wish, this may entail bringing in some unlikely classroom exhibits; if they are free to have a better idea than the teacher's, this may distort the teacher's plans for the following week.

However, the most important 'climate' of all is that which surrounds the individual child. Given the challenging nature of writing, it is easy to give children the impression that while many are called, few are chosen: you will all do it but only a tiny minority will succeed and be rewarded. Each child will only have faith in his ideas if there is time within a busy day for them to emerge, if they are listened to, and if he is convinced that an apparently ordinary life does not imply that there is nothing to write about. It is easy to see why the most affluent children have a head start in the writing stakes: 'Can I write about our holiday in Florida?' 'I'm going to put down all about our trampoline,' and why children for whom the highlight of the week has been a trip with an older sister to the local fish and chip shop should feel that 'I've got nothing to write about'. Without doubt confidence is a vitally important agent for success in any task but where the risks are as high as they may be in writing, where the possibilities for failure are greatest, then confidence is all-important:

BN: You said you weren't any good at it [writing poems], didn't you?
Sandra: No, I'm not very good at it.
BN: Now why do you say that?
Sandra: Because when I was at primary school I got a very low mark for a poem that I'd done and the teacher put underneath it: poetry isn't your bright spark, or something, is it? And that's what put me off I think.[10]

Organization for writing

There are three major organizational options for the inclusion of imaginative writing in the primary curriculum: individual, small group and whole class work. Writing may occur whenever the child and teacher feel it appropriate, as so often in infant classrooms, the writing to accompany or precede a picture, the jotting down of ideas while the thoughts are there, the 'Can I write about it?' response to a piece of drama, television programme or trip. This option allows both teacher and pupil to introduce a writing activity when the moment seems right; the writing is likely to be more motivated and individually tailored, less run of the mill and predictable. Such *ad hoc*ery inevitably makes considerable demands of the teacher's time and skills, given that at any one time, while some children are writing imaginatively others may be engrossed in quite different activities. The teacher cannot always intervene, question, listen or suggest at the best possible time since her attention is divided between so many individuals. Children may be left twiddling their thumbs, or worse, while they are awaiting teacher. The ideal, of course, is that individuals would have sufficient autonomy and confidence to initiate their own ideas unaided, with the teacher as consultant after the bright idea, if not before.

Small groups of writers may emerge spontaneously: 'We all want to write a book about life in the future . . .,' or may result from a teacher suggestion or directive: 'What if you and Alan team up with these two, to pool your ideas?' 'I'm going to make you three responsible for the sports pages. . . .' The last case might assume that the whole class is working on the newspaper simultaneously, or as and when time and group motivation allow. Writing groups can healthily demolish the notion of writing as a painfully solitary activity; ideas can be shared, interests and expertise can be exploited and responsibility can be spread. Of course these groups will not be setted, that is homogeneously organized according to ability, but may be based on friendships or interests. Intervention may, nevertheless, be necessary where individuals become over-dominating, or where 'friends' are going through a difficult period. Groups should not solidify over long periods without good reason, in the interests of the cross-pollination which is encouraged when children work with a variety of colleagues.

Whole class teaching, that is where all the children are individually and simultaneously engaged in the same activity, has the advantage of focusing all the energy of the class, including that of the teacher. Insensitive whole class teaching has rightly been castigated for treating children as though they were a homogeneous mass with identical needs and interests. The Victorian image of the elementary class teacher standing centre front, informing pupils what they were to write about and in what way, is obviously totally out of place in any classroom which wishes to encourage diversity and creativity, but an enlightened use of whole class teaching methods can beneficially encourage corporate endeavour, class solidarity, and an atmosphere which favours composition. We all need oases of quiet and calm in which to think, and in many inflexible box classrooms the only way to guarantee such peace may be through having children working simultaneously on the same, or similar, task. The whole class approach has obvious advantages for the teacher too, since she can concentrate on a single main activity, investing her energies in lesson and resource preparation which will benefit the whole class, who may all be responding to the suggestions made in a television programme or may produce an interesting range of poetry, all of which is alliterative.

Of course, no successful teacher will dogmatically champion only one of these models. We know that the first is more commonly found in the infants classroom, and the third is more prevalent in the junior section, and that where children are grouped they may not be exploiting all the collaborative opportunities offered by small group work.[11] It may be that teachers of infants could beneficially borrow a little more whole class teaching from their junior colleagues, and undoubtedly some junior classrooms would benefit from more true group work. But it is clearly ludicrous to impose an organizational model, or even models, for writing with little or no thought to the nature of the task and the needs of the individuals. Flexibility must be the key if we are not to skew our aim to help and interest all the children, and if we are to avoid arbitrarily excluding kinds of activities merely because they will not fit into our organizational scheme.

If we take the case of a new class and a new term, where are we to start? We could ask the children in the first week how they best like to write since this is a question that needs to be asked, but it is likely to bewilder the majority, particularly if they misunderstand the terms of the question. It would seem more sensible to experiment with a provisional organizational pattern for imaginative writing and evaluate this after a fair trial.

One possibility is the writing workshop. This is probably best allotted a particular time or times in the week, if only to preserve it from encroachment from other curriculum areas. Here the assumption is that all the children will be engrossed in writing or writing-related activities, including reading, taping, discussion and art work. The classroom will be organized with these activities in mind, but immediately problems arise since, as with professional writers, the need for silence, a chat or a walk is determined by the task, the mood of the writer and the stage reached. However, we know that most writers will benefit from silence, or at least quiet, for composition purposes, while others will welcome the chance to collaborate over a piece of writing. The ideal is to custom build a classroom which combines the comfortable quietness of a library with the creative conviviality of a design department. Such an environment would incorporate a library and reference area, accessible materials which would resource all the writing-related activities described above, space for drama, a separate recording room, large art tables, a writing area in which collaboratively noisy work could take place, and a quiet area for solitary writing. There would be tables which faced windows and others which deliberately did not, an exhibition area which encouraged children to touch and remove articles and other, necessarily static displays. Children would move from area to area at will, signalling to their colleagues the kind of activity they were contemplating.

In primary schools such custom built workshops are unfortunately rare; most of us do however manage a compromise. After a session in which all the class have been trying to write simultaneously in a classroom which has not been modified with writing in mind, it is well worth asking the class the question: 'How could we change the room to make it easier for you to write?' Such an inquiry might profit from the teacher sharing her own thoughts about her own ideal writing environment, so long as these do not deter pupils from making their own views clear. The responses may result in a creative, if modest, foray into classroom design and decision-making: What can we do with what we have? What could we import? Will we need any workshop rules? If so, what will they be? How will we organize and dispense the materials we will need?

Behind all these questions lies one fundamental one: what will the role of the teacher be? We will want to answer several essential needs, to signal to the children that writing is something prestigious, creative and enjoyable, in short something that teachers also do. We will thus also write during workshop time. We will also want to be accessible so that children can, where appropriate, seek our aid or try out first drafts. We will also need to be all-seeing, unobtrusively monitoring who is doing what, with whom, nipping problems in the bud, reprimanding the inconsiderate and on occasions spurring on those who need it. To do all this we must be mobile. Clearly, we cannot sensibly be consultants and writers simultaneously, so a *modus vivendi* has to be negotiated between teacher and pupils, just as it must between pupil and pupil. The teacher too must be able to signal, 'I'm now, like you, moving to *my* quiet area, at my desk, and writing. I expect you to treat me with the consideration I do you when you are in your quiet area, and only disturb me in an emergency.' This does not preclude the fact that, when deep in thought, we are also scanning the classroom, controlling and monitoring through our gaze. In the early days the expectations can be reinforced by 'Please do not disturb' signs, which teacher and pupils can display on their desks. Children seem to find such ideas fun, and they give writing a self-importance it otherwise might lack.

No teacher can appropriately monitor or counsel children if she is reeling from one trivial request to another: 'Can I sharpen my pencil?' 'I've forgotten how to spell "Tuesday" again,' 'Martin called me a pig and you said. . . .' No child can concentrate on composing, reviewing, transcribing and editing if he risks falling victim to similar comments from his peers. Thus children should share in the process of deciding how such problems can be minimized. They need to answer questions such as, 'How shall we organize our materials so that everone knows how to collect them without bothering the teacher and so that everyone gets their share?' 'What do you do if you need to know how to spell a word?' 'What do you do if you're not sure what to do next and the teacher has her "Do not disturb" sign up?' Trivial requests are likely to wither where children know that the teacher does not condone the telling of tales, will not tolerate inconsideration, will not allow children to become over-dependent, and will distinguish between a perfectly sensible request and the spurious 'reflex' one. Thus an underconfident and hard-working child who is concerned about the layout of the final draft will receive sympathetic help, while the perfectly capable but sluggish child who has been disturbing his neighbour and then fusses over the layout of the first draft may be firmly reminded that layout is not the essential concern with first drafts, and that he would have made greater progress if he had not been wasting his time, and that of others.

Once organized and negotiated, the writing workshop has much to commend it; it dignifies writing with a time to call its own and fosters the conditions in which writing is most likely to be successful. If we believe in 'Uninterrupted, Sustained, Silent Reading', then there must surely be opportunities for USSW: 'Uninterrupted, Sustained, Silent, Writing'. The workshop should cater for the child who wishes to continue to write his great opus alone and silently, while somehow finding the space for those who wish to use improvisation or art and craft as a accompaniment to writing.

However, one or two workshops a week will not be enough alone to cater for those bright ideas which bubble up between. Children, like all writers, will need to be able to lay down ideas as they occur, often inconveniently, in the midst of other activities. For this they will need a jotter, rough book, or better still the equivalent of the author's 'commonplace book'. Children may make these books entirely their own by making all the decisions associated with their production, the size, colour, weight of paper, covers, the width of or lack of lines, the illustration and binding (the more professional the better). Some may choose to experiment with transfer or stencil lettering, with different coloured pencils or inks, with illuminated letters and numbers. Others may legitimately see their book as a wonderful 'amnesty' space where the teacher has no automatic right of entry and certainly no right to correct or complain; a few will exercise their right to refuse to keep one. Almost invariably children do want the teacher to see at least some of the pages in these books, and sometimes a written dialogue develops as the child asks questions which he wants the teacher to answer: 'Do you know a book about witches?' 'I want to write a letter to my friend who's in hospital – will you help?'

Ideas will not bubble up if children have no investment in their writing, no reason for caring about tying ideas down while they are still red hot. Clearly, the teacher cannot and should not attempt to force children to note good ideas, but we can make it more likely that they will want to if we too keep a commonplace book and share our finds with the class, whether interesting phrases, idioms, verses or words, when the moment seems right, and equally allow children to take the stage to entertain the class with their findings.

Writing for an audience

From time immemorial pupils have thought, and latterly said, 'I don't know what to write about,' 'I don't know where to start,' 'How long does it have to be?' and 'Is that enough now?' Most professional writers also ask such questions, but in circumstances more conducive to writing than those encountered by many pupils. Teachers have been, somewhat unfairly, berated for apparently inviting such comments, when they are, unfortunately, the quite routine stress or deflection symptoms which are manifested by all writers, at one time or another. Many writers will understandably lean as heavily as they can on an apparently concrete requirement in the otherwise frighteningly nebulous world of composition. The writers of most romantic fiction, for example, have some quite strict conventions for guidance, and have in mind a clearly delineated audience and target length.

We can minimize these stress symptoms by making it easier for children to answer such questions for themselves. Taking the first pupil statement above, 'I don't know what to write about,' we must first weigh its significance according to the circumstances in which it is said. The astute and lazy pupil may conclude that it is easier to lean heavily on a teacher who will comfortingly prescribe a subject than to think for herself, particularly where that teacher's expectations of the pupil are artificially low and where a perfunctory piece of work will do. But in a classroom where children are encouraged to demonstrate initiative, to think before they ask, the question may signal, 'I know what I want to write about generally but I can't find the right angle, or way in,' or, 'I've got so many ideas that I'm bewildered by the choice but please don't prescribe for me because I'm still at the thinking stage and I'll make up my own mind if left a bit longer,' or 'I've got so many ideas, my brain's overloaded, please put me out of my misery and make a suggestion (even if I then reject it) since I need something to hang on to,' or 'I know what *I* want to write about but I don't think you will approve.' Clearly, responding to such requests sensitively becomes easier as we come to know our pupils better, but, as with all aspects of teaching, we need to maintain a balance between 'Teacher know thy pupils' and ensuring that our knowledge does not become solidified into the kind of rigid expectation which leads to labelling, and hence the self-fulfilling prophecy. Children need the 'head room' in which to demonstrate their potential and pleasantly surprise us.

'I don't know where to start' may be a deceptive statement, since it may have more to do with insecurities about the length and ending of the piece than about the beginning. As when approaching the bus station, we need to know our destination before we can discover the appropriate departure point, thus 'I don't know where to start' may really be asking, 'Who is this for?' and particularly, 'How much do I need to tell them in order to make myself clear?' or, 'How long can I make it since this will decide how much detail I can afford to include at the beginning?' The statement may also hint, 'I don't know what kind of writing this is going to be. I want to write about a train journey but will it be a description of my journey, a whodunnit or a hold-up?' The statement may indicate that more, or less, time for thought is needed; more time conceivably where the child has felt rushed into writing, perhaps by the apparent diligence of his friends or by an inquiry from the teacher, or where he has rushed in unspurred in order to finish as rapidly as possible. Less time for thought may be beneficial where the rush of words, almost any words, on to the page may allow the writer the option of rearranging these or rejecting them in favour of better alternatives.

Having in mind a specific, interested and discerning audience removes some of the fear associated with composition. Writing for a single audience, in a classroom where spelling, punctuation, handwriting and neatness appear to count for more than the quality of the content, encourages the kind of conformist mediocrity in which neatness is next to godliness and where it is dangerous to experiment with long, interesting, and probably misspelt words. Alternatives to the teacher as audience can be divided into two main kinds, the real and the notional. Real audiences for writing include fellow pupils in school or in other schools, parents, pen pals at home or abroad, school staff and indeed anyone who might appreciate a notice, story, report, poem, magazine, book, poster, script, and anyone who could be addressed in a letter: letters in response to articles in the press, in response to advertisements, letters to celebrities, other writers, local radio stations and politicians. The opportunities are limitless, and the excitement and suspense generated by the wait for the response makes the effort worthwhile. Replies can be read, displayed, responded to; relationships can develop as photographs are exchanged, opinions are shared and questions are answered.

Those local audiences to be found within the school or home

are in some ways the most valuable of all, since they can be easily consulted; their reactions can be most immediate and, most usefully, they can participate in the composition process. Thus the junior age child who wishes to 'write a story for the infants' can consult the target reader or readers in order to determine the kinds of stories they prefer. This may be demonstrated when the audience asks the writer to read a favourite story with her, or for her. This valuable symbiotic relationship may result in the infant child returning the favour with products of her own. The child who wishes to discover what it means to be a member of the ancillary staff may, with permission, seek the views, perhaps the writings, of relevant personnel in order to produce 'A Day in the Life of our Caretaker' or 'What Does a Dinner Lady Do?'

Inevitably not all classroom writing will be directed at 'live' audiences; that does not imply however that all remaining writing will be intended directly for the teacher. Notional audiences usefully encourage the child to anticipate the needs of the particular reader, even where that reader is unlikely to materialize. Thus the writer may imagine that he is describing what it means to attend his school, or play the game of football, or visit a British seaside resort, as if for a pen pal from another planet, thus ideally encouraging that decentring process in which the child begins to envisage the needs of an audience, beyond himself. Inevitably such notional audiences imply a modicum of role play; the child is imagining he has an alien pen pal, or is replying to someone from another age, or is providing a description for someone who cannot see. The permutations proliferate when the writer too enters into role, perhaps looking at twentieth century technological developments as if, like Woody Allen in the film *Sleeper*, he has awoken from a previous time, or writing as if from the point of view of one of the many outsiders in society.

Such empathic understanding does not come easily, and should not come glibly. There is a huge difference between saying and writing 'poor old man' in the classroom and resisting the temptation to join in the onslaught when one's peers insult an elderly vagrant in the street. Drama can help to deepen the understanding by embedding the writing in action and speech in role. Some will object that infants, in particular, are still likely to be at the 'egocentric' stage and thus may be incapable of sustaining a role in writing. It is true that the role mask is likely to slip as younger children transfer their own wishes and characteristics to the part, but this is not invariably the case and to talk of readiness for rigidly defined writing stages is as dangerous as outdated notions of reading readiness. In short, we are unlikely to be surprised by what children can achieve if we do not encourage them to have a go.

Demystifying composition

Given writing's reputation, we need to try to dismantle it, talk about it, play with it, in short demystify it and promote it as a craft, rather than as an aesthetic mystery. Many children, like many adults, have fanciful notions about how inspiration comes to 'real writers', based, one suspects, upon vestigial visions of effete poets being rocked by inspirational trances on Cumbrian fells. Talking to real writers, including real poets, is usually a consoling process. They generally confirm that writing is often a messy, bitty, lengthy, sometimes serendipitous, but just as frequently methodical activity, and one which anyone can do, since a writer is someone who writes.

We can contact our regional arts association in order to invite writers into the school, but often writers 'emerge' once an interest in writing is established. Even a small village will generate a surprising number of writers, some in print and some yet to be discovered. So long as their work is intelligible and suitable and they can discuss it in a stimulating manner such visitors have much to contribute to childen's understanding of the ways in which other writers work. Their very lack of celebrity can be an advantage, actively demystifying writing and bridging the gap between the pupil and the professional. They may have more opportunity to work alongside children, teaching at times by example. At a time of high unemployment, writing has a significant part to play as a creative leisure activity; there is seldom a shortage of those who are willing, interested and free to involve themselves in the classroom workshop.

So many children (and teachers) seem to have tacitly accepted the assumption of 'straight into best' writing by the time they leave the primary school, thus adopting a straitjacket that no professional writer would accept. The neatness factor, particularly apparent to girls, then compounds the problems associated with composition, since if writing must be right first time and look as perfect as possible, messy creativity is stifled by a concern for surface features. Children need to see the apparently inconsequential doodles, the untidy crossings out, the many pieces of paper, the arrows, the margin annotations that adults use, and which are such valuable aids in the composition process. They will be too young to make much of Ezra Pound's redrafting of 'The Waste Land' or Blake's several versions of 'The Tyger', but they deserve the opportunity to explore some of the perhaps less subtle changes made by a visiting writer, the teacher, or their colleagues. At the very least, the teacher can display the changes he has made to a piece of prose or poetry, with a particular audience in mind. The changes needed may be brazen or amusing, a thank you letter which is inadvertently rude, the inclusion of some gross contradictions; or may be more subtle, the over-use of certain words, tautology or ambiguity. We may demonstrate to pupils the various stages our own imaginative work went through, from doodled ideas, through untidy drafts, to final polished version, and should be brave enough to ask which of the drafts they liked the most. This should indicate that 'redrafting' is merely a compendium term implying many composition processes: the rearrangement, insertion or rejection of existing material. Obviously a word processor, or its microcomputer equivalent, is a valuable and for many novel aid in this process, but failing this a felt board, magnet board or overhead projector all facilitate the manipulation of words and can demonstrate that redrafting can be a tactile and graphic activity as well as a cerebral one.

We cannot afford to assume that children will accidentally assimilate redrafting techniques; we need to be prepared to intervene to demonstrate how redrafting works and how it can help in the composition process. To this end, we may have to deprogramme the single draft practices of the past, by sharing writing problems with the class: 'I wrote this story for my niece who is your age, but I got fed up with it and screwed it up. Later I thought, perhaps it's not all bad – and I wondered if you would help me to decide what to keep and what to get rid of. . . ,' 'I want to enter this short play for a writing

77

competition . . . but I'm only allowed 1,500 words, so parts will have to go. . . ,' 'Scott has asked for your help – this is his poem but he thinks there may be something wrong here – he'll tell you all about it.'

Children understandably equate redrafting with tidying up the surface features of spelling, punctuation, handwriting and layout, or with the tacking on of extra bulk, usually at the end of the piece, hence their inquiries, 'Is that long enough now?' 'Have I got it right now?' All writers have to learn, sometimes painfully, that some parts are best omitted or that it would be more helpful to backtrack to the last section of the writing which was successful, rather than piling on mediocre material at the end.

Redrafting is not something which happens as a second-rate postscript to composition; it is composition. Until the moment of finally going to press there will be opportunities to change the content. When compared with the redrafting of content, the copy-editing of surface features is of lesser importance and can be delayed until the last moment, once the content is in place. We may need to be aimiably ruthless with those children who find it difficult to break the habit of equating redrafting with copy-editing and insist that they stop worrying at details of spelling and punctuation, in a few cases even banning them from looking up or asking for spellings until the penultimate draft is complete. We can best help children by demonstrating the split between composition and transcription; we cannot afford to take this to the privileged extreme Barbara Cartland does, dictating to an efficient secretary, who then takes responsibility for transcription, but there are other and cheaper devices. Children can talk through ideas, plots, stories, which will never be fixed in writing but may be published in a different form: on audio or video tape, through dramatic interpretation, through a cartoon or series of slides, thus rewarding those with vibrant imaginations whose transcription skills are weak, and allowing them the success which might otherwise be denied. Some might suggest that such children require extra practice in spelling, handwriting and punctuation, and this is true to an extent, but an over-obsessive concern with these features will penalize these children and draw attention to a failure rather than highlighting a success, and reinforce the false image of the good writer as the neat and accurate transcriber.

It is tempting to dismiss redrafting as merely the latest of many language bandwagons, as a nostrum persuasively peddled by American academics who are safely removed from the daily wear and tear of an overcrowded classroom. Redrafting devours classroom time, and paper, and may, if not carefully managed, reduce the teacher to an exhausted wraith. If redrafting is synonymous with composition, it is also closely allied to assessment, for it assumes that someone will weigh up the qualities of the draft before deciding whether or not changes are needed. In an ideal world the child would effectively appraise his own work, seeking advice from no one, beyond his own objective criteria for excellence. In such a world there would be little need for teachers and classrooms. In reality, the best guide and most proficient writer in the classroom will be the teacher; to deny this fact or to withhold our professional help from pupils amounts to a denial of our role. To give too little guidance will leave children floundering and will invite chaos, to give too much will discourage the very autonomy and creativity that we seek, and not least will reduce the teacher's role to that of instructor. If we invite children to depend upon us for making even the most trivial decisions, we shall be left doing little more than answering peripheral questions about transcription matters: 'Can I start a new piece of paper now?' 'Julian says he won't lend me his rubber.' If children know that such distraction tactics are open to them, they will quite naturally use them to interrupt the difficult process of composition. (It is a little like leaving a restless author alone with a television set and a full fridge.) They will saunter inconsequentially around the classroom, in search of teacher, leaving a wake of disturbed colleagues. If this is happening we need to decide whether this is the result of a spoonfeeding policy, in which case that policy must change, or whether the distraction tactics are signalling: This work is boring/I'm not sure what is expected of me/You didn't explain carefully and clearly enough at the beginning/You've given the impression that accuracy is the highest priority and I'm bad at spelling.

These problems can multiply in classrooms where redrafting is encouraged, for here work may go through several versions, each of which may require the teacher's appraisal. If she is not to disappear beneath a scrum of anxious children, some decisions at least must be delegated to pupils. The maxim must be, think first, if you cannot immediately answer the question, and if the circumstances are right, consult a colleague or a reference work. Only if this strategy fails, and there is no obvious alternative, seek the help of the teacher, but only when she is not helping someone else. Children need to demonstrate restraint, tact and responsibility, if redrafting is to be successful.

There is a danger that in avoiding the 'straight into best' writing policy we may fall prey to an equally rigid approach to redrafting which then becomes just another teacher imposed chore, lacking any rationale or value. Redrafting needs to be exploited in a flexible manner; some very successful writers hit pure gold seams of single draft writing where the astute author and editor will recognize its excellence and leave it well alone. We must be prepared for young writers who produce what we consider to be an inferior second draft and then tell us that they prefer this one, and for disagreement among a group which is trying to edit its own publication. Most importantly, we cannot expect redrafting to achieve anything if the child does not feel any sense of investment in the writing in the first place.

The transcription skills

We learn most rapidly and effectively when we are most motivated to do so. Motivation is a key factor in mastering the transcription skills of spelling, punctuation and handwriting; it is only worth spelling words correctly or punctuating work if the writing interests the child and if the audience appreciates this attention to details. Both these elements must be present; a teacher who cares about spelling accuracy does not guarantee that the child will care equally. If this was the case pupils would not produce the dozens of spelling solecisms, the results of a lack of care rather than ignorance, that they do. Conversely, a writer who is interested in his work may choose not to bother about spelling errors if he feels that the audience will not mind; thus we may waive spelling and punctuation considerations when writing informally to trusted and uncritical friends.

Spelling is a somewhat contradictory business. It is a low-level, uninspiring skill offering virtually no opportunities for creativity; indeed the creative speller, who would have felt at home in the golden age of prestandardized spelling anarchy, is penalized. Spelling can be totally divorced from the composition process, but, like an accent, it can be revered by society as a touchstone for the writer's educational attainment, even his state of mind. The majority of proficient adult spellers are unremarkable; it is the weak and inconsistent speller who brings attention to himself with mistakes such as these: 'I wood be gratefull if you could send me the necessary articals before Wensday. . . ,' and one wrongly placed letter can reduce a serious intention to laughable bathos: 'The old lady said the old man was unbareable so she locked him up.' In such cases it is important to distinguish between slips where the writer has not bothered to weed out misspellings of words he can spell correctly, when challenged, and fundamental ignorance about letter-sound relationships and spelling patterns. Between these two poles is the grey area of non-standard, but phonetically logical spelling attempts, spred for spread, littel for little, which in many cases are relative successes, rather than failures. The 'grey area' of spelling approximations is the orthographical equivalent of the young speaker's attempts to generalize from what he hears: 'I runned all the way home,' 'What have the gooses eated?' They are also the equivalent of the progressive approximations in conformity to text of the young reader, and as such are to be commended and built upon, since they suggest a thoughtful attention to sight-sound correspondence. Thus the child who has just acquired the confidence to use the word 'weather' but has spelt it 'whether', far from being penalized, should be praised; there will be ample time to explore these two spelling possibilities later.

Fundamental spelling errors, that is those which are not the result of inadequate checking but which suggest an ignorance of letter-sound correspondences, and thus will not and cannot respond to reminders to 'check your work carefully', suggest a range of possible problems. The child may have poor visual recall of words; he may have difficulty in discerning typical spelling patterns; he may not be able to hear properly or sound out the words properly; he may be of low verbal intelligence and may even have brain damage. Additionally, he may have suffered from inadequate teaching or the over-teaching of spelling. Given this range of possibilities, clearly diagnosis, though often difficult, is the necessary first stage in helping to solve the problems of the habitually poor speller.

Although research into the teaching of spelling tends to produce some apparently contradictory advice, it can be helpful in suggesting principles which will determine the way spelling is taught:

1 Spelling proficiency is closely linked with motivation and the child's self-image. If labelled a poor speller, he will tend to conform to this label.
2 Spelling is best taught bearing mind the particular needs of the individual. Any spelling instruction should have direct relevance to the child's own writing needs; only useful or interesting words should be taught.
3 Little and often is better than an exhaustive and sporadic approach. Children with particular spelling problems need short, regular periods of practice which build confidence through experience of success.
4 Pupils should be encouraged to see the patterns in words (for example, the '-ate', '-ry', '-ill' families), and to divide longer words into syllables and focus on the most difficult syllable before reinstating the word as a whole.
5 Where spellings are provided by the teacher, this should be done in writing and never letter by letter, in order to encourage visual recall. The child should then be encouraged look, cover, remember, say, write and check the word.
6 Mechanical copying, as in 'Corrections', is usually ineffectual in teaching correct spelling since the child is not encouraged to analyse the structure of the word.
7 Children should be given ample opportunities for practising their new spelling acquisitions, in their own written work, rather than in arid spelling tests.

Individual children will, like adults, have problems with particular words or kinds of words. There will be the child who finds 'ch' words difficult, or who has problems with the final 'e' on words like 'gate', and there will be the many who confuse common homophones such as 'to, two, too' or 'sea, see'. Spelling, like punctuation, is best taught, wherever possible, *in situ* and in context as the need arises. Only one child may be confusing 'f' and 'ph' so it is a waste of time and effort to sentence the whole class to practice in this. Quite often, however, the same problem will mushroom in the work of several children, in which case to teach all as individuals is equally wasteful. Here the short and sweet session, which takes children back to first principles and looks in an interesting way at spelling patterns or mnemonics, is likely to be more memorable and effective than the hurried word over each child's shoulder.

But what of the child who is finding spelling (or punctuation or handwriting) particularly difficult? Won't dealing with his problems in context fail such a child? Shouldn't he be spending extra time completing exercises on those aspects of spelling which are causing the problem, using any of the many course books which are designed for this purpose? Teachers know only too well that there is no necessary transfer from these limited gap-filling skills to other more meaningful contexts, where extended prose is involved. Children who will, quite happily and almost passively, insert 'their/there' correctly in a stimulus-response manner, will later apparently obliviously confuse these two in other writing. Children who are spending too much time on these kinds of exercises are being deflected from the essential composition processes which accompany the generation of imaginative writing. It would be grossly unfair and positively unproductive to see open-ended writing (much like self-chosen reading books) as a reward for the most able, and dull exercises as the penalty for being a poor speller.

If exercises are likely to be of little long-term use, there are other spelling aids which can be exploited. The association of interesting and useful words with their graphic representations can make both parts of this partnership more intelligible and memorable. The practice of labelling work, pictures, exhibits and objects clearly and attractively need not die out in the junior years. The labels will ideally be pupil designed, and executed with their purpose and audience in mind. Attention can be directed at commonly misspelt words through displays which focus attractively on problem syllables or letters, the 'r' in February, the suffix '-ful'. Children can devise and display their own spelling flow diagrams which explain the process to be followed before resorting to the teacher's aid. Pairs or groups can concoct their own spelling mnemonics which, in their witty and imaginative invention, almost invariably surpass the existing ones. Groups can devise 'Rhyming Dictionaries for Poor Poets', which bring attention to common spelling patterns and inevitably disclose some fascinating facts about the etymology of the English language. These can be extended through a look at words from other languages which also rhyme, and can result in some novel cross-cultural poetry. Spelling 'families' can be metamorphosized to the extent where family members develop distinct personalities which suggest something of their meaning: the 'Ear' family (Ear, Dear, Fear, Near, Hear) which, with the aid of dramatic improvisation, leapt three-dimensionally from a colourful poster to introduce themselves to the rest of the class; and the 'Eat' family (Eat, Treat, Seat, Neat and Heat) who nearly came to blows in the course of a picnic.

So much valuable work can be based, however loosely, upon dictionaries. There has been a recent proliferation in dictionaries for different ages and purposes and, capitation permitting, children should meet as wide a range as possible: picture dictionaries, first dictionaries, spellers' dictionaries, a first thesaurus and, not least, children's own dictionaries, containing words which they find interesting or useful. Children need not stumble into dictionaries, coming upon the right word by chance, if at all. They can come to discover how they work by producing their own, from scratch, answering questions like, 'How shall we arrange it so that the reader can find words quickly and easily?' 'How shall we distinguish between homonyms like glass (container) and glass (transparent substance)?' and 'How much of the "man" collection (man-eater, manhole, man-made, manpower, mantrap ...) shall we include?' Inevitably, such considerations can helpfully and incidentally introduce the parts of speech in a meaningful context, not (as so often) in a vacuum where such labelling has little apparent use for the child, but as an answer to a real lexicographer's problem.

It is easy to become over-obsessive about punctuation *conventions*, since this is all they are. While spelling is standardized, punctuation is not, thus there are almost no hard and fast rules, as different publishers' and writers' practices demonstrate. It is little wonder that children become confused when told that 'Sentences always end with a full stop', when they compare, 'the man ran down the street.' with:

The man ran down the street, shouting for help as he went.
The man ran down the street; his feet hardly touched the ground.
The man ran down the street shouting, 'Help!'
The man ran down the street – I thought I knew him.
The man ran down the street and the old lady tried to follow him.
The man ran down the street but he could not escape.

The truth is that linguists cannot agree on what constitutes a word, let alone a sentence. One authority tentatively suggests, 'All that is being claimed is that the sentence is the largest unit *recognized by the linguist* as being *capable* of accounting for the range of grammatical classes and structures which turn up in a language.'[12]

Those of us who feel secure in our own definition of the sentence (a complete thought/that which contains a subject and predicate/a unit of sense containing a main verb) would do well to remember that any such definition is firstly limited and secondly complex, and hardly helpful to those who are still trying to make sense of that unpunctuated babble called speech. The child will not understand the teacher's directions for punctuating a sentence correctly unless he has already grasped the sophisticated concept which lies behind these directions, in which case he is probably punctuating correctly already and risks being confused by the teacher's formal explanation. Teachers have been heard to complain, 'He can't even write in sentences yet,' as though that was the starting point for punctuation skills and creativity. Usually they are referring to the young writers' habit of stringing units of sense together in a single breathless narrative, at best tacked together with 'and's, 'then's, or commas, at worst devoid of any linking device. Just as young writers tend to borrow the colloquial and anecdotal style of the speech they most commonly hear, so they mirror the improvised and unpunctuated nature of speech in their writing.

While misspelling can alter the sense, and make the writer appear foolish, as in, 'the dark and windy knight crept up on the house,' unconventional punctuation usually leaves the sense intact and does not dent the writer's reputation. The average reader scarcely registers 'sentences' which are joined with commas, rather than semi-colons or conjunctions, and can and does have to make sense of direct speech which is not enclosed in inverted commas. Secretaries, in particular, have been progressively simplifying punctuation, to the point where teachers of English must appear to be the last custodians of the elaborate punctuation of addresses and double inverted commas. Punctuation is less an aid to the writer, who may sensibly waive anxieties about punctuation in the haste to fix content on paper, and more of a route-finder for the reader, a courteous confirmation that the road he has chosen is correct. The reader will almost invariably make sense of the writing without this guidance but his job is made easier and quicker if he can refer to punctuation along the way. Of course punctuation can avoid ambiguity, particularly in legal documents, and Shakespearian scholars have debated hard and long the validity of editors' punctuation interpolations. But these are the exceptions; for the most part punctuation is a minor consideration in the writing process.

Since the great majority of children are unlikely to assimilate the punctuation conventions through reading, these have to be taught. They are best introduced in response to a need or an inter-est, rather than being imposed through a series of vacuum-packed exercises. If learning about punctuation is to be meaningful it must also be memorable, and thus fun. Writing down lists of teacher- or course book-dictated rules is clearly not synonymous with learning; those who already know the rules will probably freewheel as they write down what they already know, and those who do not know will never learn from copying down statements such as: 'Proper nouns must have capital letters.' 'A question mark must come at the end of a question.'

Punctuation marks can be anthropomorphized through art displays, and more vividly still, in action. A group of juniors decided to bring punctuation to life through drama. They devised a narrative line which underpinned the improvisation:

Clarie Comma was having great fun splitting up all the people at the bus stop. There was Mr Jones, Miss Higginbottom, Mrs Stevens, Daniel Davis and lots more. Suddenly Freddy Full-Stop came up and said, 'I'll put a stop to this, and he lay down on the pavement to stop Clarie Comma. What's all the fuss? said Queenie Question-Mark.

Why are you two always fighting? Stop asking daft
questions, said Freddy Full-Stop, it's none of your business.
Of course it's my business to ask questions, said Queenie
Question-Mark. Just because you're strong you think you
can beat up little people like Clarie Comma. . . .

In this case the associated display poster followed the drama,
providing a useful classroom *aide-mémoire*, associating the
punctuation marks with these distinct personalities and their
particular functions.

Victor Borge's wonderfully comic 'phonetic punctuation' can
inspire similar classroom approaches, where children associate
different punctuation marks with different noises, tones, and
lengths of sound. They can have fun reading out their writing,
inserting these sounds and experimenting with dots and dashes,
brackets and paragraphs. They should not be penalized for
over-using recent acquisitions, such as the exclamation mark,
question mark, or underlining. They may choose to write with
punctuation uppermost in their minds, rather than as a minor
consideration, thus indicating clearly to the reader precisely
how the piece is to be read. This can be tested out in
performance. Bright colours and oversized marks might be used
to amplify the writer's intentions.

It is salutary to discover how many children associate
'writing', not with composition and creativity, but with
handwriting and, as a corollary, how many associate quality in
writing with neatness and accuracy. All children need to be
helped to form, and later join, letters in a fluent and legible
manner, but this does not of course imply a rigid house style,
and should not be muddled with writing proper. Children will
and should be allowed to express their own individuality
through the style or styles they eventually settle on. In these
post-Freudian days, it should hardly need stating that the 10
per cent or more of left-handed writers should not be made to
feel aberrant but should be helped to sit, and hold writing
implements, in a way which minimizes their problems, in a
predominantly right-handed world.

It is easy to eschew doctrinaire attitudes towards certain
areas of the curriculum, while being unaware of their existence
elsewhere. It is not unusual to find teachers who claim
adherence to 'individualized' learning methods but paradoxically

insist on rather barren weekly whole class handwriting sessions, where the material to be copied is chosen by the teacher. Children should not, as in the bad old days of mass produced 'fish hooks', have to copy out a piece which is unintelligible or boring, or both. Handwriting needs to be taught systematically, and there are helpful manuals[13] which describe the options for this, but a system is not synonymous with the formal exercise. We may, just as well, and twice as creatively, exploit the moment of transition to final draft to encourage the writer to care about the final presentation and legibility of his work. As authors and poets we need to be at least fluent writers, so that we can forget about the formation of individual letters in the interests of pinning down content as rapidly as possible. Just as the reader who attempts to read each letter separately is a poor reader who will inevitably lose his grip of the meaning, so the child who is worrying about the configuration of every letter when writing an early draft is deflecting attention away from the priority at that moment, the message.

Of course handwriting can be celebrated as an art form, as another handicraft where, for example, the work may seem to invite a more italic style, the illumination of key letters, or the use of particular colours. The child may choose to write with such embellishments in mind: 'This is my Mum's favourite prayer, can I write it out properly on card for her?' 'It's supposed to be like that, sort of old-fashioned like those books we saw in the museum.' A particular, splendidly presented and authentic-looking document may provide the starting point or linchpin in a piece of drama: Herod's proclamation of the murder of the Innocents, the 'wanted' notice for Dick Turpin's head, the faked archaeological fragment from which the group works back to reconstruct a lost civilization. Formal letters addressed to celebrities, newspapers or television programmes will provide the context in which clear handwriting and accurate spelling are courteous, and a necessity, if the letter is to be taken seriously. Just as the child needs more than one reading strategy, so he will need to adapt his handwriting style, depending on the circumstances. The child who leaves the primary school will ideally have acquired a basic fluent style from which he can diversify when the situation demands.

Assessment

There is a clear relationship between how and what children write, and their perception of the audience and the assessment which their work will meet. The teacher who appears to pay more attention to the surface features of the writing than to the quality of the content is likely to encourage a similar attitude from pupils. The teacher who fails to detect that a child is marking time, recycling stale ideas, is likely to receive more of the same.

For many children assessment, or rather 'what teacher does with my work', must seem a generally negative process, in which the teacher homes in on faults. The redrafting process does not remove this temptation to pick out the weak features, rather than the good, indeed it increases it, since there may be not one but as many as three opportunities for detecting mistakes in the child's work, so that as one is put right two more emerge in the next draft. Assessment has only one aim, to help the child to improve; if our comments do not achieve this then they are better left unsaid. For assessment can only be counterproductive if it chips away at the child's confidence. There is little point in covering the work of the poor speller with numerous crossings out, and even less in ordering him to write out each mistake three times. The mess that has been made of his work will be demoralising, as will be the implication that the gulf between his work and excellence is unbridgeable. It is better to praise features which can be built upon, and only then bring attention to perhaps two or three problems and suggest remedial action.

Assessment procedures will inevitably be child-related, rather than norm-related, since if we assess the least proficient against the yardstick of excellence, their work will inexorably be bound to fail. This will imply assessing children in the light of their previous work and against notions of their potential. At one extreme this would mean that the same piece of work, produced by children of very different ability, would receive quite different responses. The very able writer who has produced a disappointing piece of work, by his standards, is likely to meet a different reaction from the teacher than the normally underconfident child who has worked hard to produce a very similar product. The dangers here are apparent, since as soon as we begin to label children as 'successful' or 'weak', once we suggest in the staffroom, 'It's very good, for her,' there is the risk that these labels will lower the thresholds of expectation, giving the less able, in particular, the impression that they will only be expected to succeed in a limited sphere. We tread a tightrope too when we take into account the child's home circumstances; it is clearly unfair to be over-demanding of the child who has been ill or is grieving over the death of a relation, friend (or indeed family pet). However, it cannot help the child to suspend normality for too long, particularly where this singles her out as being abnormal in some way.

Different kinds of work will demand different assessment procedures, many of which will not be administered by the teacher, at least initially. Take the case of the editorial panel of children who are ultimately responsible for the production of their own magazine, and who have commissioned a colleague to produce a particular kind of article, of a fixed length. They, and not the teacher, must assess this article's worth, although their criteria for selection will ultimately be assessed by the teacher, as will the commissioned work. Children will valuably envisage alternative assessors and audiences; the story written for the younger brother or sister will be appraised in its true context, at home, but the teacher will be quietly monitoring progress, praising and making helpful and tactful suggestions at appropriate moments, and taking the trouble to inquire if the younger child enjoyed it.

Very personal writings, particularly those which help to exorcize unhappiness or grief, clearly cannot be assessed in the more objective way that more detached writing might be. Few teachers would be insensitive enough to pick out spelling mistakes here, but instead would wait for the child to signal his own feelings about the work. Conversely, humorous work deserves the laughter of an audience (where the writer agrees) rather than a mere 'Very amusing' from the teacher, while persuasive writing needs to try its skills out on an interested or uncommitted audience.

The most productive forms of assessment take place in the presence of the writer or producer, while changes are still possible, and not after the final draft, when suggestions come too late. Wherever possible, the assessment process should be shared and delegated, so that children come to borrow the teacher's appraisal approaches for their own purposes, adopting those active questioning techniques which encourage the writer to move from a subjective to an objective frame of mind, to dissociate himself from private concerns with the work long enough to look at it from the reader's point of view: 'Have I told him enough for him to understand why I felt like this?' 'Have I given a clear enough description so that she can imagine the scene?' 'Is the ending convincing?'

Some assessment will inevitably take place outside the classroom, with the writer absent. Such assessment is of course generally described as marking, which implies far more than the simple ascription of a mark. It subsumes correction, the putting right of that which is wrong, and thus has acquired particularly negative connotations in the minds of teachers and pupils alike. Marking, like all other forms of assessment, needs to praise wherever possible, offering children a blueprint for future success: 'I particularly liked the scene under the railway arches Michael – I could imagine it easily – has this ever happened to you?' Immediately the limitations of marking are apparent; much of the vocabulary of literary criticism (vivid, convincing, realistic, persuasive) is nebulous and often unintelligible to young readers. Such problems somehow dissolve when meanings can be explored and amplified in the presence of the writer, who can ask and answer questions, seek advice immediately, and, perhaps most important, describe the intentions which underpinned the work.

Marking demands a policy all of its own; it must be intelligible to the reader. Squiggles and abbreviations which have meanings for the teacher are likely to be as confusing as hieroglyphs to the child. Where we wish to provide the right spelling for a misspelt word, rather than ask the child to check the spelling later himself, this must be legible and written in full, as close to the original word as possible. *If* the work is to be given a mark or grade, this must have some meaning. What does 6/10 mean? Is this related to his previous work? What has he achieved in order to earn 6? How has he lost 4 marks? Even more confusing: what does a grade C mean? Is that close enough to A to be good, or close enough to E to be poor? Is it average, or mediocre? Will the child only discover by referring to the work of all his colleagues? Marks and grades are so invidious and arbitrary (and, significantly, encourage the child to focus on the mark alone, rather than on the all-important comment) that there seems little point in using them for imaginative writing, in particular.

Whatever the form of assessment, we will need to be aware of our aims and of the criteria for success, and share these with each child. At a simple level this may mean clear exposition at the beginning of an assignment: 'I'm hoping that you'll be able to persuade the rest of us that we shouldn't bulldoze the wood, so you'll need to attack each of our arguments. . . .' More subtly, and more valuably, children will be invited to decide the criteria for success for themselves: 'Well, we've only got three minutes, and we've got to fit in all this news, so we'd better make sure only the important bits get in. . . .'

Classrooms are stressful and competitive places; pupils feel constantly assessed and seldom off-duty once they have entered the school building. They deserve oases, amnesties from assessment, and particularly the freedom not to produce a final draft, the right to say, 'I know the spelling's wrong but I just wanted to read it out,' 'I don't want anyone to see it,' or 'Don't write anything on it – I like it how it is.'

Allied to assessment are monitoring and evaluation, the ongoing and retrospective appraisal of the extent to which our pupils are achieving our and their objectives, and equally the appraisal of the efficacy of our own teaching methods in facilitating this. Both require the keeping of records, so that important data is not lost and is acted upon, and in order to provide a more long-term profile of the child's progress or lack of it. Of course such a record exists in the child's writing, and Her Majesty's Inspectors have indicated their disappointment that this living resource has not been more generally exploited:

> Surprisingly, in only about a third of the classes were samples of children's work regularly used to monitor progress. In fewer than half of the classes was children's own written work used as a basis for teaching spelling, syntax, sentence structure or style.[14]

Checklists can be used to build longer-term profiles of the child's progress, but while they are convenient in that completing them is usually a quick and simple process, this very simplicity can result in a straitjacket which can have wider implications. Checklists inevitably have built in assumptions and generalizations; the tend to cut down each child and each piece of work to a similar limited size. They conceal a semantic problem too; what do words like 'originality' and 'organization' mean? How does any checklist come to terms with notions like appropriateness of register, or writing in role, which may require the product to be fluid or tightly structured, hyperbolic and even deliberately boring, on occasions? Instead of, rightly, reflecting a stimulating curriculum, checklists may begin to determine a more pedestrian one, in which children are pushed into particular kinds of writing in response to the perceived demands of the checklist. Such lists or grids almost invariably place the emphasis on *product* rather than *process*, when it is the latter which may decide the long-term success of the writer. They seldom consider the circumstances in which the writing came about, the ambitiousness of the task and the initiative of the child, the planning and redrafting involved, the social skills demanded by collaborative work, the responses to sudden problems, the exploitation of aids and materials.

Checklists and other formal assessment cards, however all-embracing they may seem, are always limited and fallible since writing (like talk), quite rightly, has an inconveniently creative habit of defying watertight categories; a diagram may convincingly appear in the middle of a story, a character in a play may quite logically break into verse. We might wonder how we would do justice, on a form, to the child writing in role as a medieval chronicler who is recording the reactions of the local populace to the unexpected collapse of their cathedral spire. An absurdist writer, and there are many budding N.F. Simpsons and Ionescos in primary schools, will go to some lengths not to be constricted by the conventions of any one literary genre, striking out in any direction which seems suitably anarchic at the time. One wonders what a checklist would make of the wonderfully inventive and surreal talents of Laurence Sterne, James Joyce or Spike Milligan.

The law of diminishing returns operates with any form of assessment sheet; the fuller they are the more likely they are to record accurately the written output of any child, but the more comprehensive they become the greater is the teacher time which will be spent completing them, time which might better

93

be spent on other teaching activities. And, as with all diagnostic procedures, assessment sheets of whatever form are only valid where they result in appropriate remedial action, where necessary. Identifying the problem is merely the preamble to finding a solution.

Monitoring procedures need to be sufficiently broad and flexible to accommodate all the processes and products of learning. The teacher's journal or evaluative record book, meticulously kept, offers such flexibility, and in its freedom to report on the processes, provides an important adjunct to the records of products, contained in children's work. The journal is best written up regularly, at least once a week, and so as to ensure that the unobtrusive and self-effacing are not pushed aside by the noisy extroverts, each child should have a reserved space. Broad sub-headings are helpful in preventing the comments becoming too nebulous and anecdotal (for example, Reading, Writing, Talking/Listening, General/Misc.), but many comments will cut across such boundaries, and go beyond them. We will, sadly, not be able to immerse ourselves in these records in quite the same way Michael Armstrong was able to do when he documented, in journal form, a year spent in a class of 32 8- to 9-year-olds:

> Paul, after telling me about his go cart adventures, was keen to commit them to writing and settled down to the task with his usual concentration, by turns earnest, pensive, pained, listless, and sometimes all in one. It took him all morning and the last sentence I had to write for him, as his scribe, but the thought was his own. The piece that emerged was more assured than much of Paul's writing despite the limits of length which his present technical ability imposes on his pieces. [15]

We can, however, find the space and time to pin down perceptions which emerge in the course of looking at and working with children:

> Robin's writing which *follows* a picture, model, television programme seems more assured than that which precedes, or stands alone.

Ian wants to sit alone to write a 'secret story' – find a niche.

Paramjit has blossomed as video director – must have more leadership opportunities.

Have tried not to notice Mark's sillinesses, seems to be doing the trick and he loses interest too. Perhaps I nag too much.

Such records demonstrate the links between pupil monitoring and the evaluation of our own successes and failures. It is so easy to shut down success for children by failing to provide the context in which they can demonstrate their talents, or by expecting too much too quickly, or through insensitive help or comments. Neither failure nor success occurs in a vacuum, and just as we can take some credit for our children's successes, so we must evaluate our part in their failures.

4

Routes into writing

The list of ideas which follows, though limited, aims to indicate a selection of starting points for discussion, drama and writing. And, as children frequently demonstrate when they collaborate to devise new ideas, one central theme will always breed many possible variations.

1 Spider Plans and Segmenting

These help to reveal writing possibilities by dividing global subjects into more manageable proportions.

The home

The inhabitants

Figure 4.1 Segmenting

96

2 Elaboration exercises

These, like segmenting and spider plan approaches, aim to disclose the possibilities latent in enigmatic starting points. Here the base is a simple sentence, for example:

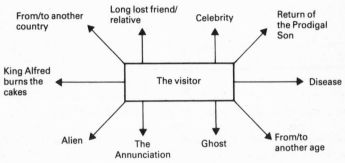

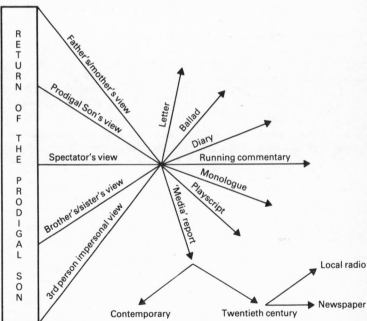

Figure 4.2 Spider plans

(A) was invited to meet a stranger and the meeting led to unexpected results.

All the content-laden words can then be challenged:

(A).. was invited................................

who?/what?	when?
appearance? age?	by whom?/what?
personality? background?	how? why?
opinions? ambitions? (etc.)	

to meet....................a stranger..................and the meeting led

when? where?   who? (etc.)

to unexpected results..

what?
when? where?

Children might first attack the teacher's sentence and then devise their own, passing them as challenges to other pairs or groups. When more than one group is stretching the same sentence, the finished elaborations can be interestingly compared. While ideas can be aired and shared through pair, small group and whole class discussion, perhaps leading to more extended writing, the answers can be most fully developed through dramatic improvisation which discloses many more possibilities, through the interpretation of events and characters, in time and space.

3 Plot models

Many young writers know of only one plot model, the chronological ordering of personal experience, with all the first person advantages and disadvantages that this implies. Children need help in diversifying from single models, through hearing and reading stories which take other forms, and exploit other narrative devices. Some young writers will tread the path of the development of the English novel from the dream devices and animal fables of Chaucer and his contemporaries, through the pseudo autobiographies of Defoe, the imagined letters of Richardson, towards the picaresque tradition of Fielding and Smollett. All these are accessible plot models for inexperienced writers, and all have been exploited by children's writers. Beyond these are the variations, many of which are familiar from fairy tales and fables:

- Transformations (for example, 'Beauty and the Beast' and 'The Ugly Duckling').
- Tests and challenges (for example, 'The Three Little Pigs' and 'The Princess and the Pea').
- From real life to fantasy (for example, 'magic carpet' tales and 'The Lion, the Witch and the Wardrobe').

To these can be added the plots that emerge from real life and the media, the undoing of the vain or foolish (so wonderfully exploited in Shakespearian comedy and in the *commedia dell'arte*), the events unleashed by rivalry or revenge, or by mistaken identity. Children can discover and explore several manifestations of the same plot, in the newspaper article, television programme and family life, and in literature from other ages and cultures.

4 Writing recipes

These expose the nature of particular literary genres by
itemizing typical ingredients. Thus for a science fiction
story/novel/play/screenplay/poem the writer might collect:

> One inventive and evil scientist
> One or more inquisitive and preferably rash leading
> characters
> An innocent population – slow on the uptake
> An incompetent police force

A suitably cooked ghost or horror story might require:

> A stranded traveller
> An isolated castle
> The sinister owner of the castle
> A sympathetic or sinister servant
> Multifarious, yet to be explained, noises

A conventional melodrama (basic recipe) might demand:

> One scheming villain/ess
> One hero – thoroughly good, but easily fooled
> One heroine – innocent, beautiful and vulnerable.

To these can be added recipes for typical romances, farces,
westerns, and fairy stories. Such recipes open up opportunities
for the analysis of plot conventions and assumptions. Discussing
these ingredients with children reveals the extent to which sex
stereotyping, if unchallenged, will dominate young writers' own
plot construction. Most will assume that the scientist is male,
that if there are two leading characters and one is female that
she will take a subordinate role; and the second recipe above
often results in a story which has entirely male characters, or
merely a nominal, rather feeble, maidservant.

These typical plots have embedded within them conventions
concerning the ways in which the action will progress.
Commonly the ending will be a happy one; good will triumph
and the hero (and heroine) will live to fight another day. But
plot development is only possible where the villain is initially
more clever than the sympathetic characters, or where these
make one or more costly early mistakes. If the piece is to end

happily a reversal is required before the dénouement; the sympathetic characters may stumble upon some good luck or some vital information, the villain may become over-ambitious or careless. If all else fails a *deus ex machina* may intervene to dispense poetic justice and restore equilibrium.

Some children will enjoy hearing about the medieval notion of the wheel of fortune which decreed that the leading character, once at the top of the wheel and thus most fortunate and apparently secure, was also most vulnerable, since progress was inevitably downward to misfortune. The familiar see-saw provides another graphic representation of possible plot development: Thus, in a melodrama for example the play, poem or story may begin with the heavyweight villain forcing the lightweight hero or heroine to crash to the ground. However, against the odds the hero raises himself to that moment of equilibrium which provides the suspense in the penultimate scene, in which either good or evil could triumph, before forcing the villain down to a fate which will be irreversible.

5 Pictures as starting points

While there are numerous paintings which explicitly illustrate a story (notably many Pre-Raphaelite works and some of those by Hogarth and Brueghel), many more pictures and paintings are less overt but nevertheless indicate several possibile narrative threads which can be teased out and developed. L.S. Lowry's industrial scenes respond well to the kind of careful and ever closer attention which reveals private conversations, public events, family outings and intriguing outcomes. Children, working as a group, may inquire:

What is happening beyond the artist's vision?
What has just happened – or is about to happen?
Where is the artist in relation to his/her subjects?

The group may focus on a sub-group, unseen spectator or the artist, and enter into role in order to expand a particular scene or viewpoint.

6 Person, Place and Thing cards

Person, Place and Thing cards are at their best when produced by the class (and vetted by the teacher, to ensure as broad a sweep of permutations as possible). Each category should have its own distinctive coloured slips of paper or card, which will be placed face downwards, or folded. Individuals, pairs or groups then choose one from each category, to reveal often surreal combinations:

the lollipop lady   –under the bed   –a giant panda
William the Conqueror–Blackpool Tower–a banana sandwich.

While a few children will prefer to work individually, keeping their interpretations secret until the last possible moment, most will welcome the chance to discuss how best to incorporate these elements into a story, improvised scene, play or poem. On occasions the group will decide to jettison one of the cards, and so long as they are not evading the challenge prematurely, this is part of the kaleidoscopic fun of the game.

Children are adept at suggesting their own variations on the Person, Place and Thing idea, for example:

- the random selection of articles, all of which must be incorporated in some kind of narrative;
- a variation on the Advent Calendar, where different doors reveal a variety of characters and objects;
- a card game where the winner has only one card from each set of categories in his hand at the end of the game, and must then tell a convincing tale involving this combination.

7 Basic plots

Older children, at least, can begin to explore the differences between the plot and the more elaborated and manipulated story, by recounting, as simply as possible, what happens in a tale they know well. This is quite a demanding task and some examples may help to suggest what is required:

A family of three go out for the day. While they are out a visitor explores the house and leaves mysterious signs of the visit.

('Goldilocks and the Three Bears')

Two young children are cruelly sent away from home. They have many adventures before reaching safety.

('Babes in the Wood')

Such simple but effective plots can be transformed by setting the events in the present or in the future, by shifting them to another country, or by translating them into those languages spoken by children in the classroom. The plot can be radically changed by switching the gender of the leading character: 'Alec in Wonderland' would probably be quite a different book, as would 'The Iron Woman'.

Children may wrongly equate plot distillations like those above with stories, and thus assume that there are no more decisions to make, that the writer simply proceeds from the chronological beginning to the inevitable end. They can perhaps best be helped to see that the very simplicity of these plots opens up a diverse range of interpretations, by confronting the questions which any screenplay writer or film director must face:

What kind of a film shall we make?
For what kind of audience?
Which of the characters will be at the centre of the action?
How shall we make this clear to our audience?
Where shall we start – at the beginning of the events, *in medias res*, or at the end, and then flash back to the beginning?

A group of children might start with a plot they have devised, or borrow a familiar one, for elaboration:

A young girl sets out to visit a relation. She arrives, unaware that the relation has been attacked and that the stranger she finds in the house is dangerous. With some help, and through her own quick thinking, she saves herself and her relation.

('Little Red Riding Hood'[1])

The group may have been asked to imagine that they have been commissioned to write the screenplay. They must ask, and answer, all the production questions, similar to those above, which will decide the nature of the finished film. But of course the screenplay will only answer some of the questions; if the group is invited to make the film they will soon realize that even the most precise screenplay still allows a great deal of creative scope and decision-making to the director, actors and editor. Fortunate children can produce their own video interpretation, experimenting, for example, with camera angles to gauge their effects: 'Should we show her face as she goes to the house, or her back?' 'What if we don't show the stranger's face at first but only hear his voice and see her face?' Where the video equipment is not available, drama can be a viable alternative, as children act out different versions and invite their audience's comments and preferences.

8 Same events: different viewpoints

Before and after

This approach takes as its starting point the assumption that if a play, story or novel is to convince us, we must believe that there is life beyond the confines of the pages, that is, that the characters have a past and conceivably a future, that when they leave the scene or chapter they have somewhere to go and something to do when they get there. For example:

- What happened before the beginning of the Cinderella story which caused the Ugly Sisters to become such domineering creatures?
- Did Cinderella and the Prince live happily ever after?
- What were the Three Bears up to while Goldilocks was trespassing in their house?
- What sort of a day had the innkeeper in Bethlehem had, before the arrival of Joseph and Mary?

By reangling the viewpoint adopted by the original author children can come to see the contrived nature of any writing, and particularly fiction. The writer has chosen to identify with one character, but might equally well have written the account from an alternative viewpoint. This can be particularly effective where the writer identifies with a less sympathetic, or minor character. (See, for example, Jean Rhys's *Wide Sargasso Sea*, a memorable reworking of *Jane Eyre*, which focuses on the early life of the first Mrs Rochester.) A final authentic veneer can be given to this writing where the author adopts the style of the storyteller: 'Miss, he's a giant, he never went to school so he can't use long words and he spells things his way. . . .'

Such approaches of course are not restricted to story telling. Children can explore the ways in which perceptions of real events are inevitably coloured by the nature of the witness. This might involve focusing on a report from the local paper or local radio:

DANGEROUS LORRIES STORM

Residents of Blackfriars Road are today claiming that recent accidents there are a direct result of the increasing number of heavy lorries which are using the road. On Wednesday a pupil of the Blackfriars Primary School suffered leg injuries when. . . .

Children may choose to identify those who may have witnessed the events, and those who are likely to have an opinion to present, and may compare possible statements from those involved. This may develop into a dramatic reconstruction of events, from different points of view, resulting conceivably in newspaper and local radio reports which differ according to the nature of the reporter, the viewpoint of the witnesses, the type of newspaper or radio programme and the target length of the report.

9 Plot trees and flow diagrams

With or without computer programs designed for the purpose, children can explore plot permutations with the help of flow diagrams or plot trees. The idea of the branching plot is familiar to many children through the proliferation and popularity of 'game' books, in which the reader can choose (or throws a dice to decide) one of several plot sequences. While teachers have understandably criticized the poor literary quality and aggressive masculine tendencies of many of these books, they are useful in suggesting the myriad options for plot development, particularly where a new land or a dangerous journey is involved.

Children who do not have access to a microcomputer for displaying their plot trees will need plenty of space and paper, since at each stage the number of options doubles.

One day x discovered a tiny door set into an overgrown bank at the bottom of the garden. x decided to open the door:-

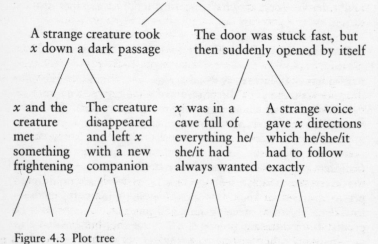

Figure 4.3 Plot tree

Of course it is not the intention that children should passively accept the teacher's or the computer program's plot suggestions, though both may provide a temporary prop or launching point. To feed children a recipe and then expect acquiescence is to destroy at least half of the opportunities for creativity, since truly imaginative writing depends on the nurturing and pruning of the writer's own ideas. So many children think of writing as a response to the ideas of others that it is important we emphasize that thinking and planning are vitally important writing processes. Thus, children may devise a flow diagram (see Figure 4.4 pp. 108–9) or plot tree which they then choose not to develop, or which they pass to or exchange with a colleague or group. They may treat it as a game or as an elaborate cloze exercise, in which certain parts are left blank for completion by a partner, or may exploit both as bases for drama.

10   Creating new worlds

Fantasy worlds, like science fiction, free the writer's imagination from the constraints of the real world; in both the restrictions and rules of geography, time, and humdrum realism can be defied, even if internal consistency must be maintained.

Maps for such worlds are not merely helpful guides to the reader, they are vital elements in the composition process. Most children choose to produce a map in the early planning stages, basing any subsequent writing on this. The maps can relate to imaginary lands set in the past, present or future, they may be in the sky, on an unexplored planet, under water, within the human mind, even in an undisturbed part of the back garden or attic. The inhabitants usually surpass even Swift's invention, taking on any form, shape or size, and allowing the writer fascinating opportunities for wish fulfilment. As the maps take shape, so the imaginative possibilities multiply. Few children get to the end of their first drafts without claiming enthusiastically, 'I know what's going to happen. . . .' At first a predictably picaresque plot will often emerge, but beyond this are the many other writing possibilities, occasionally written in strange new languages (with translations): the letters sent from one part of the country to another, or to another land, the messages in bottles, the newspaper and news reports (where applicable), the official documents, notices, broadsheets, poems, the official histories, even cookery books.

One child chose to produce an official, propagandist 'Tourist Guide for Moansville' (capital city of the Miseries), having collected and sent off for examples of this distinct literary genre. The finished work included apparently authentic street maps, advertisements, suitably depressing descriptions of 'Beautyless Spots', a foreword from the Misery in Chief, and some thoroughly off-putting statistics. Other children have developed their own board games based upon their imaginary

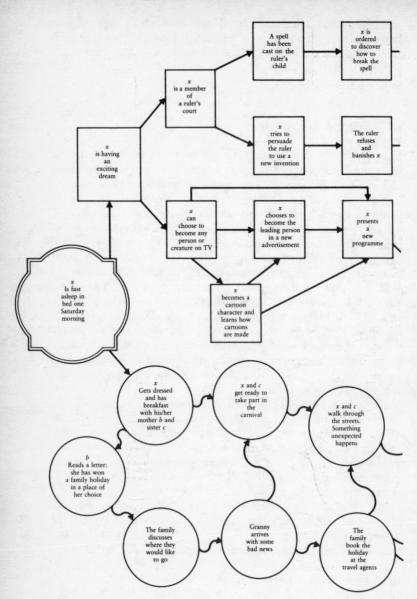

Figure 4.4 Plot flow diagram

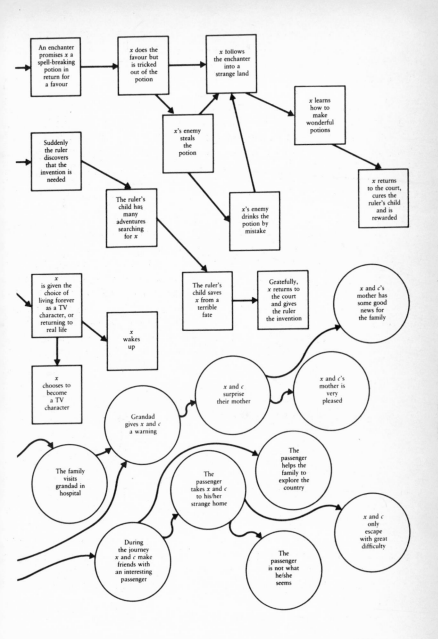

An enchanter promises x a spell-breaking potion in return for a favour

x does the favour but is tricked out of the potion

x follows the enchanter into a strange land

x learns how to make wonderful potions

x returns to the court, cures the ruler's child and is rewarded

Suddenly the ruler discovers that the invention is needed

x's enemy steals the potion

The ruler's child has many adventures searching for x

x's enemy drinks the potion by mistake

x is given the choice of living forever as a TV character, or returning to real life

x wakes up

The ruler's child saves x from a terrible fate

Gratefully, x returns to the court and gives the ruler the invention

x and c's mother has some good news for the family

x chooses to become a TV character

Grandad gives x and c a warning

x and c surprise their mother

x and c's mother is very pleased

The family visits grandad in hospital

The passenger takes x and c to his/her strange home

The passenger helps the family to explore the country

x and c only escape with great difficulty

During the journey x and c make friends with an interesting passenger

The passenger is not what he/she seems

109

Figure 4.5 The Land of Truth and Lies

110

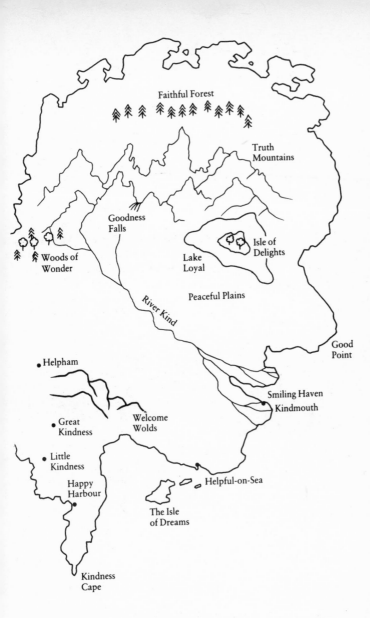

Faithful Forest

Truth
Mountains

Goodness
Falls

Isle of
Delights

Lake
Loyal

Woods of
Wonder

River Kind

Peaceful Plains

Good
Point

● Helpham

Welcome
Wolds

Smiling Haven
Kindmouth

● Great
Kindness

● Little
Kindness

Happy
Harbour

Helpful-on-Sea

The Isle
of Dreams

Kindness
Cape

lands; one example was based upon a people who tried hard never to complete a job, thus the winner of the game was the one who fortuitously collected as many delaying tactics as possible so that the game was never completed.

5

A place for poetry

The separation of this chapter is significant, for in the minds of many poetry has an exotic, somewhat arcane reputation which distinguishes it from all other aspects of reading and writing. The poet is commonly seen as a member of a rather extraordinary, even threatened, species and as a privileged soul who can afford the luxury of introversion and meditation, well clear of the routine concerns of everyday life. The *Bullock Report* candidly stated,

> It has to be acknowledged that poetry starts at a
> disadvantage. In the public view it is something rather odd,
> certainly outside the current of normal life; it is either
> numinous, and therefore rarely to be invoked, or an object of
> comic derision.[1]

One might expect teachers of English to demonstrate greater commitment to poetry than the general public, but recent surveys suggest an apparent lack of teacher confidence in poetry in the classroom. The Bullock committee found evidence of wildly different practices, from the most enlightened delight in poetry to examples of classrooms where children rarely encountered poetry at all. The 1978 Primary survey[2] noted that poetry was read by childen in only about two-fifths of the 11-year-old classes. A recent and much needed survey of the teaching of poetry[3] was inspired by the perceived neglect of poetry in the classrooms of 9- to thirteen-year-olds. In a first chapter significantly entitled 'What's Wrong?' the editors comment, the lesson 'Poetry' which occasionally appears on primary timetables is an ordeal for many teachers. . . . Faced with a curriculum based largely on the acquisition of 'knowledge' and 'skills', many teachers are insecure when confronted by a poetry lesson.[4]

Such insecurity seems perplexing, since poetry is arguably the nucleus of the 'literature' that English claims as its own; while other aspects of English are fruitfully poached by other curricular areas, poetry should be safe in its literary niche, being neither a transferable skill nor a body of knowledge. If English has no time for poetry then it can be claimed that the curriculum should have no time for English.

Yet it seems that many children, and boys in particular, feel that poetry is useless, pointless, and positively boring. While 60 per cent of the APU sample [5] of 11-year-old girls confirmed that they had read or enjoyed a poem, or part of a poem, when they were younger, only 37 per cent of the 11-year-old boys did so. The report authors conclude, 'over half of the pupils in the sample had formed negative views about the interest and value of poetry reading.'[6] A more modest recent piece of research[7] disclosed that over half of its sample of 10- to 11-year-olds could give no reason at all for writing poems and only a tiny fraction suggested that poetry writing could be enjoyable.

A good poem is of course only useless in the sense that a wafer thin priceless porcelain vase or the Mona Lisa could be said to be. Even those teachers who are wary of introducing poetry would not deny its importance, in Coleridge's terms, as 'the best words in the best order', and at its best as Shelley's single word which may be a spark of inextinguishable thought. These two great poets are mentioned here since all teachers and readers of poetry have inherited their legacy, the daunting weight of the accumulated greatness of past poets. Few who have had any literary training will have escaped without a concept of the poet which is in great part derived from the nineteenth century 'Romantics'. Thus the poet is almost inevitably male (female poets of the past are almost inevitably seen as dilettantes), white (one might assume from school and university English exam courses that poetry peters out beyond Dublin and the Channel), and somewhat agonized, even antisocial. Pain and poetry seem entwined; the notion of the well-balanced and contented poet is a relatively new one. So much has been claimed for poetry by so many influential writers (Aristotle suggested that it was more worthy of serious study than history) that it has acquired a semi-sacred status, a mystic untouchability. Once the poet has distilled his combined wisdom into a few painfully won lines, it seems churlish to do anything other than revere the effort, even if we then vote with our feet and avoid the product.

Yet poetry is all around us, in the playground, in mnemonics, advertising slogans, song lyrics, even graffiti and football chants. Rhymes feature significantly in the child's acquisition of language and many favourite childhood games are based on verse ('Down to the bottom of the deep blue sea. . . ,' 'This little piggy went to market . . .'). Young children chant and manipulate familiar rhymes as they are playing or lie in bed. There is no evidence to suggest that children leave the home to join the reception class with an ingrained disaffection for poetry and yet we know that by the time the student leaves compulsory education, and in many cases by the time the 11-year-old pupil joins the secondary school, a disenchantment with poetry has set in for life.

Perhaps we can only begin to ameliorate this situation if we come clean about our own feelings for poetry. Poetry arguably inspires more feelings of guilt among primary teachers than any other aspect of the curriculum; guilt perhaps because we would seldom read a poem unless teaching demanded it; insecurity because we feel ill-informed about current developments in modern poetry; guilt perhaps because we suspect that we only like the poems we do for the wrong reasons; anxiety because we only feel confident when introducing poems we know and love, and yet simultaneously feeling rightly wary of imposing our tastes on our pupils. Poetry poses a threat to those teachers who pride themselves on their omniscience. Great poetry cannot be translated neatly and directly into prose or into right answers, since its poetic irreducibility constitutes a part of what makes it great. I have used the word 'great' for want of a better one, but value-laden epithets like 'great' encumber the teacher and raise a host of questions. What is great poetry? If a poem recurs in anthologies does this indicate greatness? Thus, is the only great poetry old poetry, tested by time and its wide appeal? Given the demands made by a wide curriculum on classroom time, should we concentrate on the 'greats' in the time allowed to us for poetry? Is it better that a child should meet a little Wordsworth or Tennyson, even though he finds these daunting, or should these be avoided in favour of less durable poets with greater initial appeal?

It is possible that we have unconsciously conveyed a narrow view of poetry, one which focuses upon male, solemn, nineteenth century poets. The authors of the APU Primary Survey [8] noted that while children in their sample cited modern writers of fiction, many of the poems mentioned were Victorian or Edwardian. Thus there were more references to Wordsworth, Tennyson, Houseman and Masefield than to contemporary poets. The authors surmise that this reflects 'a situation in which the poetry to which these children are typically exposed tends to be somewhat restricted in type' [9] and suggest that this might in part explain many children's negative views about poetry. It is intriguing to note the contents of a recent anthology [10] which claims to be the first collection of poems to be chosen by children; while Spike Milligan, Michael Rosen and Charles Causley are included, it is interesting to discover that poets which were fed to a post-war generation still dominate the selection. It might be objected that the choices reflect the particular nature of the sample, or the preference of the compiler, but it is more likely that the selections reflect the kinds of poems which pupils typically meet in primary schools. Of course I am not suggesting that pre-twentieth century poetry should be avoided, far from it; rather that care should be taken to ensure that poetry is not associated with a rather rarefied, white, male, dead, middle class elite, and that it is seen to be alive and well and being produced by writers of both genders, of all ages and cultures, and for all kinds of audiences and purposes.

Positive discrimination

It is easy for poetry to fall through the curriculum sieve. The reading and writing of stories are safeguarded by accepted practice, teacher intervention and pupil interest. Their neglect will be noted, but the demise of poetry may go unnoticed. It is tempting to wait for poetry to emerge spontaneously from pupil interest or accidental catalysts, but even the provision of excellent anthologies will not in itself inspire childen to take the trouble to grapple with this less familiar literary genre. Positive discrimination in poetry's favour is sometimes the only way to guarantee that it finds a foothold in the curriculum. At one extreme this may mean submersion in poetry, the poetry week or day, with all its accompanying risks and rewards. It may mean setting aside the time so that teacher and children can share, though not over-analyse, poems which they have enjoyed. It may result in deliberately reading narrative poems rather than the routine story, or focusing all imaginative written work on the compilation of a class anthology. Positive discrimination may imply the exploitation of a library loan of anthologies; the preparation for and follow-up to a television broadcast, visit from an adult poet, or school or class sponsored poetry event. This is not to suggest that poetry should be segregated from other aspects of the curriculum, nor that children cannot start poetry trails of their own. Poetry has obvious affinities with other aesthetic disciplines, notably music, art and drama, but since no subject is unpoetic, poetry can gain from and contribute to a relationship with any subject, and in so doing can delight, amuse, instruct, object, describe, reply and report, in short can fulfil all the functions of prose if it so wishes.

Inevitably, none of this will be possible in a classroom where poetry implies pedestrian and predictable approaches. Its reputation will be indelibly tarnished if children come to interpret poetry thus: 'She reads us a poem and then we answer questions about it and then we write our answers down and then she marks them;' 'If we like the poem we have to read it out to the class and write it down;' 'She always reads us poems about nature and they're boring.' Ideally, children will choose to bring in poems, will suggest setting them to music or performing them, will choose to write them for parents and friends and to publish them appropriately, and will want to seek out the work of favoured poets. But such choices are not possible in a classroom where poems are inevitably teacher-chosen and inexorably laboured over.

A way of working

In the literary wake of F.R. Leavis and I.A. Richards. poems have become conveniently packaged, cheaply duplicated fodder for the 'New Criticism', which favours the hermetically sealed package of literature which can be torn from its context and analysed word by word. Once the analysis is complete the student has earned the reward, an opportunity to suggest what he liked or disliked about it and why. Such practices have crept from the ivory towers of Oxbridge English departments into primary classrooms, passing through examination courses along their way. In shifting attention away from literary history and crude linguistic analysis, these approaches have been helpful, but they have also, unfortunately, given the impression that the good poem is the poem that responds well to the word-by-word analysis. Such poems are typically dense with figures of speech, cluttered with examples of alliteration, metaphors, similes, hyperbole and personification, which can be comfortingly noted. Other poems may be relegated to an inferior position, or even ignored since there seems little to do with them.

The teaching of poetry demands a delicate balancing act which combines careful attention to the nature of the poem with a sensitive concern for the particular audience. Some poems are so immediately accessible to the whole class or group that they are best read expressively, enjoyed and passed over relatively quickly. Other poems may entertain some children, despite the fact that every word or line is not understood, particularly where the rhythm is strong, the word patterns are satisfying, or some participation is encouraged. Other poems may depend for their appeal on a very personal identification with the subject matter, perhaps the death of a pet, the annoying habits of a brother or sister, or a trip to a well-loved place. There will be some poems which children come to appreciate only after they have been helped to unlock possible meanings, perhaps through group discussion or a working out of the ideas through art or drama. This is worthwhile where the challenge is within pupils' reach, where the analysis is not over-extended, and most importantly where pupils feel the poem has sufficient intrinsic appeal to justify the effort. But we have to come clean here too, for it is easy to assume that because we have been moved by a poem it is worth pushing children through the poetry pain barrier for the deferred fulfilment of appreciating the poem at some later stage.

Positive discrimination must extend to convincing children that poetry is not a painful inoculation but is fun and often funny, can be disposable, and need never be taken too seriously. This last comment deserves some elaboration, since all successful poets, even the most apparently frivolous, do take their work very seriously. 'Seriously' in the classroom context quite often means assuming that the poet must be right, that his or her words are immutable, that they have been arrived at as the result of sudden inspiration, and not least that the poet understands what his or her poems mean. Inviting professional poets into the classroom can be both a liberating and a consoling experience. Modern poets typically demystify their *craft*, which is precisely how most see it. They usually admit to the messy drafts, the scribbled notes and the sometimes extended gaps between writing one line and another. They seldom present pat answers to questions like, 'How did you come to write this poem?' 'What does this line mean?' and are sometimes even brave enough to confess that the dictates of the rhyme scheme decided the content of certain lines. Meeting 'real' writers demonstrates the ridiculousness of asking children to write single draft poems, the foolishness of expecting them to turn on feeling to order or in response to a perfunctory stimulus, and the sensitivity which is demanded of the sympathetic audience who may be responding to a poem which has a therapeutic and cathartic function for the writer.

A way of looking

Poets commonly refuse to see themselves as eccentric, other-worldly creatures. Most agree with Ted Hughes[11] that the writing of poetry does not require particularly dramatic experiences, nor a huge vocabulary, but rather distinctive ways of looking at the world. The most successful of modern poets, in particular, seem to share a refreshing and surprising view of life. They may take conventional subjects and find oblique and unusual approaches,[12] or launch into perversely and often amusingly unusual subjects.[13]

Such originality can be nurtured in the classroom by exploring possible approaches to the topic chosen, and by encouraging the kind of identification with the feelings and experiences of others which is so apparent in the work of Langston Hughes and Roger McGough, in particular. A conventional subject like 'A Walk in the Park' can result in a poem which is refreshing just because it refuses to meet its reader's expectations, perhaps written from the point of view of one of the squirrels which must share its domain with a variety of strange interlopers called humans. A humdrum subject like 'Holidays' can be brought to life if the poem switches to the future, to imagine a world where the inhabitants are so bored with enforced leisure that holidays constitute welcome periods of intensive work. The voice in the poem may then be that of a visitor from an earlier era, or perhaps that of a participant in a 'holiday camp'.

Art students are familiar with exercises in ways of looking at mundane, almost invisible household objects, a fork, a carrot, a toothbrush, drawing or painting them from unfamiliar angles or in unusual styles. Young poets can borrow some of these techniques, doing the apparently impossible with the most unlikely subjects: 'Twelve things to do with an Orange', 'The Ruler Tells His Own Story', 'A Spider's Eye View of the Bath'. This kind of subject can be liberating and challenging. There are no precedents, no conventions to lean on, as with so much nature poetry; the writer can strike out without looking over his shoulder, and must find a voice of his own. Children might even nominate the most difficult subjects for poetry and then try writing very short poems about them: 'Fractions', 'A Bit of Dust', 'An Eyelash'. Many children find these easier subjects than the disconcertingly huge 'Spring' or 'Snow'. Such approaches inevitably extend the scope of poetry and, in the process, help to destroy the assumption that only certain subjects are poetic

Communal poems

We can help to destroy the myth that poets are inevitably solitary, introverted beings by encouraging children to write pair, group or whole class poetry. List poems[14] clearly lend themselves to group approaches since each child can contribute

a line, a word, or an image, associated with the chosen theme.
The finished poem may be extremely simple and uncontrived:

> *'Christmas is . . .'*
>
> Looking for hidden presents
> Saving my pocket money
> Another jumper from Gran
> Feeling stockings. . . .
>
> *'When I'm Grown Up I Will . . .'*
> Stay up late
> Eat chocolates in the bath
> Go out after dark
> Buy a stick insect. . . .

These two list poems could, if the writer chose, be partnered by
'Christmas is . . .' and 'When I'm grown up I will . . .', as seen
through the eyes of a young famine victim, or a writer from a
past or future century.

List poems take many forms; lines may alternate:

'Likes and Dislikes'
What I like about Sundays are the breakfasts,
What I dislike about Sundays are the television programmes.

What I like about my hamster is his warm fur,
What I dislike about my hamster is his awful temper.

The contributors to the poem may suggest single adjectives,
verbs or images:

> *'Wild Life Park'*
> Fat sheep,
> Wriggly lambs,
> Cows asleep,
> Angry rams.
> Deer feeding under trees,
> Hippos shaking off the fleas,
> Llama bored inside his pen,
> Cockerel looking for his hen.

'*Grownups are . . .*'
Kind,
Nagging,
Helpful,
Annoying,
Smiling,
Frowning,
Generous,
Mean,
Sensible,
Silly,

Quite important creatures.

'*Bonfire Night*'
Rockets roar,
Sparklers splutter,
Catherine wheels wobble.
People watch,
Children rush,
Rain falls,
We all go home.

Effective poems can be successfully built from invented collective nouns. Such poems can be enjoyable collaborative enterprises: writer A produces the 'heads' on the left-hand side of his sheet, while writer B produces the 'tails' on the right-hand side of her sheet. A and B then swop sheets and complete them:

Heads		*Tails*
A wallow	of	hippos
A whisper	of	grasses
A stumble	of	foals
A fumble	of	waiters
A worry	of	mothers
A wrestle	of	maggots
A scatter	of	children
A spatter	of	sausages
A sparkle	of	dewdrops
A bristle	of	toothbrushes

A conversation	of	clocks
A wander	of	supermarket trolleys
An embrace	of	footballers
An ouch!	of	stinging nettles

Children can use the cloze formula to challenge each other to complete poems, or may use colleagues as collaborators in order to resolve particular problems. A child may pass his incomplete poem to a colleague, who then attempts to make sense of it by adding appropriate words. (This is a simpler, though less exciting alternative to displaying the poem with the aid of a microcomputer.) The two or more versions are then compared and perhaps displayed together:

> '*Bluebottle*'
> I'm black and blue and hairy,
> With   big   eyes   on   my   ....,
> I'm always looking for a meal,
> 'Specially one that's dead.
>
> You'll often .... me buzzing,
> In .... mucky places,
> And when I've sucked the rubbish up
> I settle on your faces!

Children can suggest refrains for the poems of others, and exchange challenges with each other: 'Write a poem where each line has a different colour in it,' 'See if you can write one with all the days of the week in.' More ambitiously, different children may contribute 'in role' to a poem which describes a single experience from many angles:

'*The Day the Aliens Landed in Salisbury Market*'
Narrator:	One Tuesday at ten thirty,
	A strange thing happened in our town,
	The market people stopped to see
	A space craft coming down.
W.P.C Gray:	I saw immediately it was parked
	Upon a yellow line,
	I threatened to arrest it,
	Or serve it with a fine.

Mr Edwards:	At first I hid behind my stall,
(*greengrocer*)	In case they tried to shoot,
	But when I saw how thin they were,
	I offered them some fruit.
Mrs Pemberton:	Once they saw my golden chain,
(*Lady Mayoress*)	They knew that I was special,
	They offered me a guided tour,
	Around their strange space vessel. . . .

Such work may emerge from, or lead into drama; some of the most successful and satisfying group poems seem to derive from group drama, perhaps because the ideas have already been explored.

'Communal' poems can be built from a shared experience; the 'Farm Sounds' group poem, for example, which emerged from one child's realization, following a farm visit, tht cows do not go 'moo', as convention would have it, but have a repertoire of sounds, depending on age and mood. The child returned to the farm with a tape recorder and two colleagues to record what they called 'Real Farm Sounds'. They concluded:

> Cows don't go moo but sometimes they go mowww,
> 'Specially when they're waiting to be milked,
> Horses don't go neigh but when they're scared
> They go whay! and whehh!
> The mice go scritter, scritter, in dark corners,
> But only when it's quiet,
> The cats scowowow and hisss when a dog gets near,
> My boots go sloop, loop, sloop, loop in the mud.

Children may work together to produce pictorial theme poetry. The poetry may arise from a group frieze, diagram, painting, collage or model, or the poetry may dictate the nature of the art and craft work. Where the former is the case, 'broad canvas' themes allow most scope, for example: the fair, the market, the palace, the zoo, the farm, the haunted house, the space station, the Garden of Eden, the Land of Earthly Delights, the factory, the mountain, a stone age scene, Sunday in the park, a day at the seaside. Lest children begin habitually to equate such subjects with rather narrow, English interpretations, it is valuable to encourage them to stretch the possibilities, much as with any stimulus for imaginative work. These subjects can be pushed forward or backwards in time; they can cross the oceans or the universe, and can look at harsher aspects of life (almost inevitably where children choose to focus on a nineteenth century Lancashire cotton mill, or a typical seventeenth century fairground). The poetry can be tucked into or onto the art and craft work wherever children feel it is appropriate; doors may open to reveal a complete poem or verse, rhyming couplets may emerge in bubbles from characters' mouths, seagulls may trail banners in the sky, flags may protrude from the model or diagram with messages upon them. Children may choose to build a riddle frieze, where the riddles are written on doors, which open to reveal the pictures of the right answers; while others may produce their own group poetry anthologies which they then promote, much as though they were commercially available products.

Having fun with words

Positively discriminating in favour of poetry, in order to safeguard its place in the curriculum, does not of course imply that children should be made to write poems on a daily, or even a weekly basis. Manipulating words and phrases, having fun with these essential building blocks, is part of the process of poetic composition. The fun is important because the less confident may need to creep up on poetry unawares, creating a poem sometimes accidentally, undeterred by the frightening, 'I want you to write a poem. . . .'

Words can be collected: 'sharp' words, 'quiet' words, 'noisy' words, 'happy' words, 'violent' words, 'shy' words, 'messy' words. Real or imaginary words, using these categories, may be attractively arranged and displayed. Children can collect real or imaginary words which sound insulting or like endearments, without being either in reality. They may suggest alternatives to the many hackneyed, and unfair, animal insults: 'pig-headed', 'stubborn as a mule', 'silly old goat'. A nonsense collection might well lead to a nonsense insult poem:

'*Having a Firtle*'
You're a gribblesome snit,
    Well, you're a mulching old fardy,
A fardy am I? Then you're a snippelling young nupe,
      Nonsense! You don't know your turly flam from your
        widdiful proop.
I do so! You couldn't crup a dawpling if it zinged you in the
spam. . . .

Children who choose to write rhyming poems can find
nonsense words helpful, since they can be devised and altered
with rhyme in mind. Users of nonsense words are encouraged
to attend to the phonetic basis for spelling in order to ensure
that the finished work is read according to the writer's wishes:

> '*To Make a Peeble Pudding*'
> You will need:
>   1 zill of peebles,
>   ½ an urk of tilk,
>   3 grooling dabtrops,
>   A little mooly flook,
>   Firk them in a stim-ral,
>   Siddle them till prale,
>   Dibdob on a fardal,
>   Huggle them in spale.

Even adult writers have remarked upon the liberating effect
that judiciously placed nonsense words can have on the poetic
imagination:

> We noticed afterwards that people were more aware of
> words, more prepared to look for a new way of saying
> things. . . . Anyone who has ever sat wordbound before an
> empty page may find that it loosens up inhibitions in a
> miraculous way.[15]

Children may enjoy producing their own 'Imaginary
Dictionary' of invented words and in the process come to
understand how conventional dictionaries work. This may
result in imaginary alphabet charts ('A is for armupet, B is for
bizor . . .'), imaginary notices, invitations, letters or menus.

These ideas are more successful when they are bedded in a context, particularly one inspired by drama. Thus the invitation is issued because the devious inhabitants of the planet Krip want to persuade their neighbours, the Quoles, to attend the first intergalactic barbecue. Imaginary peoples and their imaginary languages seem to seep into other curricular areas: 'The Tarls wouldn't play rounders because they don't believe in hitting anything,' 'There wouldn't be any history like we've got – they think the future is the past so they don't have to write history books.'

A few well-chosen words may go a long way in the construction of a poem. This child's work was inspired by her enjoyment of Judith Nicholls's poem '*Breakfast for One*':[16]

> Little fat grey wriggly pet worm,
> Wriggly worm – fat grey little pet,
> Fat grey little wriggly worm pet,
> Grey worm – fat wriggly little pet,
> Wriggly grey pet – little fat worm,
>
> If I cut you in ha lf,
> I will have two!

This was finally displayed as a suitably wriggly shape poem, in which the presentation of the words attempted to reflect their sense:

Word games[17] can be helpful in encouraging children to
develop and display their vocabularies. The Parson's (or
Minister's) cat is a familiar starting point for alphabet games
and children can devise their own variations: 'Can we see if we
can make up a sentence where each word begins with the next
letter of the alphabet?' 'Lots of letters are words, aren't they?
A, bee, see, gee, eye, jay, Kay, oh ... We could do a chart.'
Alphabet poems are variations on the familiar acrostic:

'*Mistaken Identity*'

A beautiful young princess
Became tired of life in the castle,
Cooped up with the King and Queen,
Doing little all day, starved of
Exciting things to do.

Finally she ditched her crown,
Grabbed her oldest coat and
Headed for the nearby town.
In the busy streets and
Jostling crowds no one knew her.
Knights and ladies, common folk
Looked curiously at this stranger who
Might one day be Queen,
Never guessing who she was.

Opposite a little bakery she stopped and saw
Pastries, oatcakes, crumpets, bread,
Quickly she entered the empty shop,
Reached down the nearest loaf and quietly left.

'Stop thief!' she heard, and turning saw
The baker with his rolling-pin. He stormed:
'Unless you stop and give it back you'll meet a
Violent end.' 'Oh mercy me,' the Princess moaned,
'Why can't you see? I'm just a princess out to find
Xcitement, nothing more. I'll pay you with a dukedom.'
'You lying crook,' the baker cried, 'for this you'll lose your
    head,
Zounds – the King is hard on those who steal our daily bread!'

Children may decide to devise the sequel to this poem, perhaps with the aid of drama, improvising the scene where the king, queen and daughter meet and the princess presents her case. The group might envisage, and demonstrate, how this single incident changes the life of the baker, the princess, or the relationship between the court and the kingdom.

Children can have fun burying messages in their work:

Savage Arabella *v*ictimized Earnest *m*ost *e*venings!

'*Poem*'

Gareth Edwards *t*hought *m*oodily –
Every one understands this
Odious
Frightful
Tantalizing
Horrid
Irritating
Soppy
Poetic
Offering

Except *m*e!

'*To a Friend*'
If I could have a thousand things,
Like sweets and toys and presents,
If I could dream a thousand dreams and
Keep a thousand secrets,
Eventually I'd know the truth that
Yachts and cash to spend can
Only make a second best
Unless you've got a friend.

Patterns such as these, though constricting, may also, paradoxically, be reassuring to young poets in that some of the disconcerting range of possibilities are closed down. Since these patterns generally result in less personal poems, they invite collaboration in the composition and final display of the work.

Attention can be focused on the significance of layout in signalling the poet's intentions, through experiments with alternative arrangements for the presentation of the words.

Different pairs of children might share the same assignment: 'This poet has left this "poem" for publication, but it needs tidying up. Please make any final changes to it, if you think they are needed, and set it out properly, ready for the printer:'

The Man in the Moon has fallen in love with Venus the shy evening star. It was love at first sight one wonderful night when he noticed her shining afar. The Man in the Moon is hoping that soon bright Venus will vow to be true but she ignores his glances his moonlight advances and races off into the blue. The Man in the Moon has wandered off course, his cheeks are dripping with tears. He's quite forsaken the paths he's been taking for a hundred million years. The Man in the Moon knows that too soon young lovers will start to complain. There's no moonlight on earth while he goes off in search of a love which was always in vain.

Images

Just as interesting words can be collected, so interesting examples of figurative language can be gathered, from reading matter and day-to-day conversation. This does not assume dry instruction in the distinction between the simile and metaphor; drama, of a modest kind, can help to demonstrate the difference, where this is thought appropriate: the Similes tribe is at loggerheads with the Metaphors because the Similes insist that they are more powerful since they have more members. Madam Tin-Foil Bright Metaphor is furious and challenges Chief Slippery as a Wet Eel Simile to prove his claim. Both tribes are sent out to find as many 'members' as possible, before the final showdown.

Children may choose to construct poems, however loosely, from assembled metaphors or similes. There are many examples of such poems in recent anthologies.[18] Children who have enjoyed producing an alternative rhyming slang dictionary may also have fun collecting and compiling kennings, and both exercises may result in an intriguing private language. Collectors may be introduced to examples from Old English and Old Norse poetry:

peace giver = lady
gold-friend = generous prince
one stationed at the end of the land =
coastguard

gold-giver = lord
joy-wood = harp
journey elsewhere =
death

Equally vivid modern examples may result in a 'kenning poem'. If children are worried about launching straight into this, they can try a 'translation' of a piece of prose, or poem, ideally their own.

'Watching the Goggle Box'

There's seven of us in our family –
Dad and Mum, Gran and me,
Batty the Dog and Bert the Rat.
We live in a bungalow
With pink walls and net curtains,
Near the swimming pool.

Sometimes to talk to each other,
(Even to Bert the Rat),
But mostly we talk at
The Other Member of the family,
Who sits in the corner, never moving.
He's got four legs and a giant eye,
And when he gets annoying
We switch him off.

Dad mostly shouts at him
When the football's on,
Gran sings out of tune
With his hymns,
And Mum mutters
At the news.
Batty howls when he mentions
A particular brand of dog food
And Bert just chases his tail.

It can't be fun living inside
That dreary box,
Having to take all our rudeness,
Never knowing when they'll let you out.

131

So sometimes, when we're alone
I talk to him, politely,
Just to ask what kind of day
He's had.

'Watching the Goggle Box'

There's seven of us in our family –
Car-cleaner, shirt-ironer, sock-knitter and me,
Batty the chase-cat and Bert bald-tail.
We live in a no-stairs
With pink roof-raisers
And square hole snooper-stoppers,
Near the wave running water-grasper.
Sometimes we word-rattle to each other,
(Even to Bert bald-tail),
But mostly we speech-spatter
The Other Member of the family,
Who seat-parks in the walls-meet,
Never moving.
He's got four thigh-to-toes, a giant brain-window,
And when he gets stamp-footing,
We switch him off.

Car-cleaner mostly word-biffs him
When the team-kick's on,
Sock-knitter tune-tortures
With his church-hums,
And shirt-ironer throat-growls
At the disaster-and-rain.
Batty the cat-chaser bark-stretches
When he mentions a particular brand
Of cat-chaser stomach-stoker,
And Bert bald-tail just chases his bald tail.

It can't be joy-and-laughter
Life-feeling inside
That dreary all-square,
Having to take all our word-rubbish,
Never knowing when they'll let you world-wander.

So sometimes, when we're all just-us
I word-share with him,

Word-kindly, just to if-how-why
What kind of small-life
He's had.

Conversational poetry

Some children assume that poetry has to rhyme. While it would
be ridiculous to ban rhyme from children's poetry, given its
important cohesive and memorable qualities, we may nevertheless take care to introduce children to poems which are less
apparently contrived and, in their free verse, come closer to
familiar speech patterns:

'*Waiting Room*'

'Excuse me, have you got the time?'
 'Ten thirty five. Been waiting long?'
'Nine o' clock, I'm due at work.'
 'Know what you mean – my goats are
 Waiting to be fed.'

'What you here for? Tubes again?
You need a plumber, mate.'
 'It's a rash – Beryl says
 I caught it from the pigeons,
 And my feathers will drop out.'
'Infectious?'
 'Only if you stroke me I suppose.'

'You got a frog in your throat?
Something bigger?
You've lost your voice! Just nod.
My uncle had that,
Concrete lungs, they said,
So he swallowed a pickaxe. . . .
No, I suppose it's not a joke.'

'Jason, sit still –
You'll knock the scab off.
Read a magazine, take your mind off it.'
 'They're all women's,
 Someone might see me,
 Anyway, what d'you say in the letter?'

133

'Jason has a little problem but
We hope the doctor can get to the bottom of it.'
　'Oh Mum, you didn't!'
'Jason stop it, it'll never heal,
And you'll have to stop away from school.'
　'Right – that does it. . . .'

'Hang about, the receptionist's come back,
She's smiling, perhaps he's here,'
　'I'm sorry to inform you,
　Doctor Burke's been taken ill,
　He's a bit off colour, not himself,
　Under the weather, taken poorly,
　Out of sorts, feeling groggy,
　All at sixes and sevens,
　And he's taken to his bed.'
'Would you believe it? What a cheek!'
　'They'll throw us out now,'
'Just when it was getting cosy,'
　'Good thing the public library's there. . . .'

Many modern poets have successfully exploited this colloquial style. Michael Rosen's poetry comes close enough to normal conversation to be accessible, and yet is sufficiently shaped and intriguing to be memorable. 'I'm the Youngest in our House'[19] and 'I'm Just Going Out for a Moment'[20] are good examples of his work. Michael Frayn's delightful 'When I was Your Age'[21] works well in performance, as does his 'Supermarket',[22] and 'Horrible Things'[23] by Roy Fuller. For those who feel they can do justice to a broad Glasgow accent, Tom Leonard's excellent 'Six a Clock News',[24] is there for the performing; it is a poem which conveys a serious point in a manner which fascinates and amuses older children. Langston Hughes's intimate and moving 'Mother to Son'[25] invites reading aloud, again with something other than received pronunciation.

Children may, as a result of listening carefully to the differences between formal written and casual spoken language, choose to try their hands at capturing an alien visitor's or a baby's perception of spoken language:

'*Overheard from a Pram*'
— Wottadahlinililboy,
— Taint itsagal,
— Wotsaname?
— Emma.
— TsEmma? Atsanizename, owolsshe?
— Tsevnaharfmunts.
— Sdoanluklieku,
— Slukslikeherdad.
— Sheezegodizretair,
— Iz int ret!
— Wotzit then?
— Kinda orburn.
— Thaz rye tEmma yooplaywimyhan,
— Yawhanscovertindert!
— Duzzanmatta,
— Sheull bytu.
— Shaztoo!

Participation

Response to and enjoyment of a poem need not be a silent and solitary affair; it can involve noise, movement and music. Tongue twisters, humorous poems and any poem with a refrain or distinctive rhythm immediately invite reading out. Much of the work of Afro-Caribbean poets positively demands performance (though this should not prevent a child 'performing' these poems in his own mind). James Berry's 'Sunny Market Song'[26] has parts for separate voices and the 'Song of the Animal World',[27] from Zaire, requires children to take parts and mime the animals' movements. Less ambitious, but equally inviting, are the American and West Indian sound poems which require percussive accompaniment and music if they are to come alive. The sound poem which follows was written by a child, and resulted from improvisation with a colleague, accompanied by a cymbal and a triangle. The annotations are his own.

'*I went ona Travel*'

(You must hit something or clap your hands for bits like this — *feet*.)

135

I went ona travel,
Off on me *feet*,
Upa the *street*.   (Feet noises)

I went ona travel,
What did I *see*?
A cat up a *tree*.   (Cat noises)

I went ona travel,
What did I *hear*?
Some girls at a *fair*.   (Scared girls noises)

I went ona travel,
What did I *eat*?
Some smelly old *meat*.   (Ugghh! noises)

I went ona travel,
What did I *lose*?
My second best *shoes*.   (Tutt tutt noises)

I went ona travel
What did I *find*?
A girl who was *kind*.   (Aaahh noises)

I went ona travel,
What did I *meet*?
A snake in the *street*.   (Snake noises)

I went ona travel,
What did I *know*?
Nowhere to *go*.   (Say, 'Go home, go home')

I went ona travel,
Wanted to *roam*,
But aint nowhere so nice,
As being at home.   (Cheers)

One of the most interesting children's poetry anthologies to
emerge in recent years, 'One Potato, Two Potato',[28] and one
which generously allows teachers to reproduce its contents at
will, is devoted to what its authors describe as 'action poetry
for junior schools'. All the poems invite pupil participation and
imagination; thus one child will play the title role in the
'Doctor Doctor' poem and will prescribe for the bizarre
impromptu complaints that the class bring to his or her

surgery, while 'The Macrocosmic Bus' takes off with its diverse passengers, all of whom must provide a rhyming couplet to describe their destinations.

Poems which raise important issues

Any poem can provide a starting point for discussion, for the sharing of opinions and experiences, but some seem to refuse to be read and merely passed over and invite the final dimension of an articulated response. This does not imply that such poems are inevitably difficult or solemn; many pack a punch which is no less forceful for being gloved in humour. 'Happy Birthday, Dilroy!', for example, has a lightness of tone and a simplicity of style which appeal to children of different ages and abilities, few of whom fail to grasp the serious message at its core.

Suggested poems:[29]

'The Alien': Julie Holder (seeing ourselves as others see us)
'Me': Kit Wright (the problems caused by relations)
'In Trouble': Vivian Isherwood (family favouritism)
'In the Dark': Jane Pridmore (fear of the dark)
'Cold Feet': Brian Lee (fear of failure)
'Hurry Home': Leonard Clark (staying out late)
'The Quarrel': Eleanor Farjeon (disagreements, the painful problem of apologizing)
'First Day at School': Roger McGough (fear, first impressions)
'School': Isaac Gordon (the value of education)
'A Working Mum': Sally Flood (seeing parents afresh)
'Agatha's Trousers': Helen Slavin (hypocrisy and lies)
'Alone in the Grange': Gregory Harrison (the old and lonely, false rumours)
'My Dad These Days': Philip Guard (unemployment)
'The Production Line': Bobby Pearce (conveyor-belt pressure)
'Madam and the Census Man': Langston Hughes (bureaucracy versus the individual, conformity)
'The Cunjah Man': James Edwin Campbell (superstition)
'Happy Birthday, Dilroy!': John Agard (racialism, white stereotypes)

137

'Me, Coloured': Peter Abrahams (apartheid)
'Madam and Her Madam': Langston Hughes (servant-master
   relationships)
'Why?': Phoebe Hesketh (creation, the wonder of the world,
   science versus religion)

'The untouchables'

Last, but certainly not least, are the many, many poems which
seem to say, 'Don't break my spell, don't follow me up, or act
me out, or ask too many questions. Just read me as well as you
can and let me stand on my own two feet, unsupported by any
of the paraphernalia of "comprehension".' We all have our
own very individual lists of such poems, depending on taste,
mood and associations. Putting aside the many poems produced
by children which fall into this category, my own nominations
would include:[30]

'Lullaby': Burundi traditional
'The Ying-tong-iddle-I-po': Spike Milligan
'The Headless Gardener': Ian Serrailler
'Only the Moon': Wong May
'The Haunted Lift': James Kirkup
'Rabbit in Mixer Survives': Roger McGough
'A Centipede': Julie Holder
'Gran': John Kitching
'A Baby Sardine': Spike Milligan
'Night Starvation or the Biter Bit': Carey Blyton

6

Drama and language development

Some would object to the tacking on of drama, at such a point, in this book. I would sympathize with the objection. Drama is not just a school subject in its own right, not simply a means of self-expression and creative satisfaction, it is also a vehicle for learning – anything. Drama rightly refuses to tuck itself under the coat-tails of English, since it is an equal partner with any curricular activity, or at least should be.

Yet, undoubtedly, drama is 'tacked on' in many primary schools, equated with the school play or with the dance drama which emerges through PE sessions, associated with the enthusiast who runs the extra-mural drama club, with the dressing up in the Wendy House, or with the play reading during English time. The most recent extensive survey of drama in primary schools[1] set out to analyse teachers' views of the contribution of drama to the primary curriculum, and to identify the practical problems which teachers may face when introducing drama. The survey disclosed that,

> For every teacher who uses drama effectively, there are
> several who strive towards a better understanding of it and
> even more who remain unconvinced that they can use it to
> any extent in their work. Some have tried particular
> approaches and experienced difficulties from which they
> drew back, to rejoin those for whom drama remains a rather
> obscure area.[2]

To avoid drama at this point, on the grounds that it deserves a book to itself, though defensible, might risk seeing it fall through the curricular sieve, and would sadly deny the enormous contribution drama, as a means of learning, can make to language development, and thus to 'English'. But such an implied divide between English and drama of course misses the point that these two are in many ways inseparable, part of a continuum of language development. While our secondary colleagues may have timetabling excuses for distinguishing rigidly between English and drama, there are no such restrictions in most primary schools, where the class teacher still has a remarkable degree of autonomous control over the way in which lesson time is apportioned.

The reasons for drama's apparent neglect are perhaps part historical and part practical. Drama is a parvenu, a latecomer in the curriculum race, and certainly not part of the Victorian pedagogic impulse which gave rise to the 3Rs and payment by results. It is not difficult to explain why, for educational drama's results are not easily quantified, its importance owes less to product than to process, and its origins owe more to play and child-centred notions of nurturing the individual's powers of self-expression than to the classical curriculum, or even the traditional theatre. Drama can seem to cover a disconcertingly wide area, everything from the spontaneous role play of 'You be a witch . . .' in the school playground to the National Theatre performance. Because of its associations with play, and with the intangible 'talk', drama as process has had an unfairly low status, certainly one lower than mathematics and reading, and indeed any traditional subject which is dignified by its written products. Head teachers are not alone in perceiving an external pressure for something dramatic to show parents, some legitimation for the apparent time-wasting.

The apparently nebulous nature of drama can breed its own particular insecurities:

> Teachers often frankly admitted doubts about their own work in the areas considered here and referred to problems at both theoretical and practical levels. What should we be doing at various ages and stages? Is it possible or desirable to attempt a drama 'programme'? How is the quality of drama work improved? What sorts of material can be used effectively? What goals are appropriate in particular circumstances?[3]

When one adds to this list concerns about control, once the children are freed from the normal classroom constraints, and anxieties about the kinds of spaces and equipment required, it is not difficult to see why some teachers never quite take the plunge.

Organization for drama

We need not worry about the equipment required for drama, for children bring it with them. Almost without exception, they have the natural enthusiasm, open-mindedness, and sheer delight in the possibilities of make-believe which qualify them to enter into imagined worlds. They may not always be able to sustain a role and may become self-conscious at times, but they are not likely to object, 'That's not a parapet, it's a box,' or 'That's not the Queen of the Underworld, it's Adrian.'

An apparent lack of space is not an insuperable problem so long as there is a willingness to make the best possible use of the room available. The 'quality' of the space is important, the quantity less so. Those who have carpeted, custom-made drama spaces with lighting equipment and blackout facilities are very fortunate, and very rare; most of us have to exploit a classroom, with occasional forays into the dining hall cum gym, or into the great outdoors. The school hall is not necessarily the best space for drama, and it is seldom the optimum location for drama of an intimate or sedentary kind. Great spaces can be threatening; the child who feels secure within the classroom may find that the hall, or school grounds, far from freeing inhibitions, actually invite a cramped self-consciousness, and provide those distractions (a hanging rope, a passing wasp) which divert attention away from the submersion in role which successful drama requires. Those who have taught drama in the hall immediately after dinner know of the dangers of slippery mashed potato and errant peas, of the annoying clatter of washing up. Words seem to echo, there are too many inviting 'no-go' areas, and passing visitors may blunder uninvited into other worlds. The hall is at its best where the drama demands expansive movement, where groups need to work well apart from each other or where it provides a sanctum in which music, sound effects, or great noise can be contemplated without complaints from other staff.

141

The classroom has the advantage of familiarity and accessibility, and the obvious disadvantage of restricted space, even where the furniture is rearranged. It does however allow drama to erupt spontaneously in a way which is impossible where the hall has to be booked in advance. In exploiting the moment, spontaneous drama is often highly creative and rewarding, though not always comfortable. It demands a confident, flexible approach from the teacher: 'Let's stop and try to answer Jeanette's question. What do you think happened in the room, once Marcus had left. . . . ?' 'Tony and Simon want to *show* us how their creature came into the world. . . .' As with poetry, accidental moments, while valuable, may not be enough however to guarantee drama adequate time, and may be ultimately unsatisfying since they commonly come at awkward times, just before the dinner break, or at a time when rearranging the furniture is not really feasible. Pragmatic exploitation is best combined with predetermined sessions which can be looked forward to and, where appropriate, prepared for and followed up by teacher and children alike.

Classroom drama demands a particular kind of consideration for the needs of others from children who know that one thoughtless movement, one foolish shout, may fracture the atmosphere, or a colleague's self-confidence, and may put an end to the drama entirely. However, control problems seldom arise in drama once children are convinced of its essentially disciplined nature. Those who initially equate drama with superficially enacted kidnappings and robberies, or who divert any situation involving conflict into an excuse to hit their colleagues, seldom cause problems once the common sense rules of drama have been negotiated. Some of these will need to be discussed in advance: 'What parts of this room do you think we shouldn't use? Why?' Others will emerge as the need arises: 'When I clap my hands like this I want you to stop immediately please.' 'Gill, please tell us how you would like the audience to behave. . . .'

All primary teachers at times fall prey to notorious 'teacherisms'; drama inevitably multiplies the possibilities: 'One of the guards at the Gates of Castle Dangerous seems to have been bitten by a wasp. What's the problem Samantha?' Such pauses for thought are likely to be less disruptive where they are camouflaged by the teacher's entry into role and into the drama: 'Relief guard reporting for the night watch, sir. Your drink is waiting for you in the guard room.' Entry into role significantly allows the teacher opportunities for deepening and reinvigorating the group's understanding of and commitment to the work, through the planting of a challenging question or the introduction of a new piece of information: 'Brothers and sisters, it is too late, your plans are in vain. The news has come from the city, the gates will be shut and we are forbidden to leave. Oh what are we to do?' The teacher can recast or refocus the attention of an individual, through a judiciously, almost casually introduced comment: 'I'm putting together a report for my editor and I'd like to hear the views of . . . the lady at the back there, yes you madam, with the little girl. . . .' Such interventions are particularly valuable when they draw the less articulate and the more self-effacing into the drama, in a meaningful yet unthreatening manner.

Where performance, however informal, is considered appropriate, the audience will have to demonstrate as much concentration and control as the performers, or what for many children is the greatest reward of drama will be tarnished, encouraging antagonisms which cumulatively result in children refusing to take the work of others seriously since their own work has been accorded scant respect. The easily embarrassed, the underconfident, those whose first language is not English, need the kind of protection which is afforded by the well-controlled class which will not snigger at a mispronunciation, or become restless when the actor 'dries'.

Language development

The authors of the 1978 Primary Survey regretted their finding that 'In very few classes was drama exploited as a vehicle for the children's spoken language',[4] thus reinforcing an earlier statement from the Bullock committee, 'Drama has an obvious and substantial contribution to make to the development of children's language, and its possibilities in this respect have yet to be fully explored.'[5] It is difficult to conceive of true language development, which is the life blood of English, without drama. But, if by language development we have in mind rather sterile course book exercises, writing teacher-set compositions and reading disjointed fragments from tedious and interminable readers, then drama has scant hope of making a worthwhile contribution since it is likely to become just another meaningless imposition. However, 'Where schools or teachers stress the development of expressive and communicative powers, the encouragement of speculation and trial, planning, discussion and group effort, then drama is more likely to be found which matches or creates these challenges.'[6]

Language development depends on the child stepping beyond the confines of his own idiolect. It assumes an experimentation with other registers; a few of these may be directly relevant to life outside or beyond school, but many will have a 'relevance' which goes beyond this, to encourage those ways of seeing, ways of feeling, which may bring a child closer to exploring viewpoints other than his own. A child who only speaks as that truthful 'I', so dependent on his own, inevitably limited experiences, has access to only that 'I's' vocabularies, hedged about as they are by peer, teacher or parental perceptions of appropriate classroom, home or playground registers.

It is tempting to believe that vocabulary development can be encouraged by the kinds of exercises in which children are required to find synonyms for 'nice', or by brainstorming sessions which result in a host of 'Autumn' words on the board. But such exercises are light years away from those drama contexts which, at their best, allow children to synthesize their own ideas with those of others, to engage in role play which refuses to allow the child to fall back on stock responses, and which challenges the child to adopt the register appropriate to that role at that moment. The spontaneity of improvised drama can inspire the kind of language practice which is seldom possible where the work has been preplanned and prepackaged by the teacher. As the Bullock committee suggested,

> There appears to be an important distinction between children's language in improvised drama and that of most of their written work. The one is open-ended, volatile, and incremental in structure and idiom; the other is relatively closed and formalistic. . . . In drama an element of invention lies round every corner, and dialogue has a way of surprising itself so that nothing is predictable.[7]

Children can surprise themselves and their teacher; a normally introverted child may find that she can exploit the role of the leader convincingly and forcefully, and two children who are normally antagonistic can prove that they are able to collaborate effectively in order to argue persuasively in the interests of the survival of their community.

The language development offered through drama extends beyond the words, tones and registers employed in the drama itself, to include the talk which precedes, accompanies and reflects upon the work. This is the 'paradrama' language of negotiating, planning, comparing, hypothesizing and reviewing. Even where the task is prescribed by the teacher: 'I want you to show us how *you* would solve the problem. . . ,' 'You have three minutes in which to come up with your answer before the ship sets sail. . . ,' a significant number of questions remain to be answered. The decision-making opportunities are clearly multiplied when the task is defined by the pupils:

Pupil 1: (to teacher) We know what we're doing. It's going to be a play to make the Emperor smile. . . .
Pupil 2: What sorts of things would make him?
Pupil 3: He wouldn't laugh at our jokes.
Pupil 1: He probably laughs at queer things. . . .
Pupil 3: Like queer people?
Pupil 1: No, things that make us scared. What makes you scared?
Pupil 2: Like when my brother hid in the hot cupboard and made weird howling noises. . . .
Pupil 3: That's no good, he knows he's safe. Perhaps we could show him some of the funny things humans do. . . .
Pupil 2: Like watching TV.
Pupil 1: Eating spaghetti . . . having a wash. . . .

The language which follows the work, whether performed to an audience or not, is no less important than that which precedes or accompanies it. This is the language of evaluation, which children and teacher use to interpret and assess their own work, and that of others. Evaluation encourages talk which questions, infers, justifies, commends, persuades and compares: 'I think it was clever the way the man from the past kept asking questions so that the modern people had to explain carefully why they did these things,' 'We think the first one was better because it made the dragon seem more frightening, so we're going back to that one. . . .' Those who have performed may retain their roles in order to answer questions from an interested audience: 'Why didn't the old man just tell him that he'd come to the wrong place?' 'How did you feel when you saw the flowers had gone?' The audience too may have particular roles, much like a studio audience: 'I've got a chicken farm in the village, and I want to know what'll happen to my chickens if they make that runway any longer?' 'We think it's time you listened to our ideas, instead of making up your mind on your own. We do all the work and sometimes we can see what's wrong. . . .'

Language development in practice

The examples included in the remainder of this chapter attempt to describe some of the ways in which drama can help to contribute to language development, and to the integration of English, as a subject:

'Miracle Plays'

This drama programme emerged from a junior class's search for medieval England in the locality of the school. A chance question from a child, 'What did they do in the evenings?', prompted an inquiry into medieval entertainments, and thence into medieval theatre, which of course revolved around religious themes acted out in the church, streets or countryside. The class was eager to reconstruct a typical performance and, having explored the options, it appeared that the recreation of booth performances of the biblical miracle plays would ideally allow small groups of children to specialize in the presentation of particular events.

However, the transition from class to medieval actors seemed too great a single leap; an intermediary stage was needed, and offered through the recreation of a medieval community, which turned to acting to perform the miracle plays for the feast of Corpus Christi. The children decided their medieval identities and roles with the aid of a library loan, a visit to the local

146

museum, and relevant educational broadcasts. Each craftsman and woman discovered as much as possible about their particular skill, whether baker, weaver, fletcher, tailor, goldsmith, candlemaker, butcher, carpenter or shipwright.

The casting meeting, involving all the ward and guild members, was made as authentically medieval as possible. A suitable selection of Bible stories was made, ranging from the Garden of Eden to the Resurrection. Wherever possible, the skills of the participants decided which story they would take responsibility for, thus the goldsmiths chose the Nativity, with a particular emphasis on the Three Wise Men, the shipwrights happily launched into the building of the Ark, and the tailors set about the story of Joseph and his coat of many colours. Gender was completely disregarded; a boy who wanted to become the local wool-spinner cheerfully became a garrulous Mrs Noah, who owed something to the traditional Dame of pantomime, and a girl played Jesus and efficiently multiplied one stale loaf and a herring into sufficient to feed the multitude (and offer samples to passing spectators).

In order to capture something of the, often light-hearted, flavour of the original miracle plays, the children read, performed and taped adapted extracts from the Wakefield miracle pageants. These demonstrated the importance of improvising around the bare facts provided in the Bible to produce a version which was less solemn, more human, and thus more entertaining. The sub-groups responsible for depicting a particular story became semi-autonomous repertory companies, employing a director if they wished to, casting any remaining parts, voting themselves appropriate medieval wages, and determining how they would go about constructing their story. Since the class had already discovered from their researches that they were almost entirely untutored and illiterate, recourse to paper and pen was denied, although each group was allowed to nominate an appropriate figure as a 'scribe' who could make use of a piece of chalk and a board.

As convener and priest, the teacher was empowered to bring the groups together for a plenary rehearsal, to check that nothing too inaccurate or sacrilegious had crept into the performances. This allowed ward members to comment on the work of other groups and to offer helpful suggestions. Thus it was suggested that God was perhaps a little too visible, that

Joseph might have been a little more surprised by the arrival of the Three Wise Men, and Mary's accent was just right: 'She wouldn't talk poshly, would she, she was only from a little village.'

The final performances took place on the school playing fields; the 'booths' were marked out by home-made bunting, and the whole school was invited. The players performed continuously, much like old-fashioned cinema programmes, only stopping to answer questions from their audiences in the intervals. This had the incidental advantage of allowing God to perfect his homily to Noah, and the Good Samaritan to become increasingly caring in his treatment of the unfortunate traveller. The performances, while successful and apparently enjoyed by players and audiences alike, were merely the pinnacle of a much greater and engrossing programme of work, whose development had been discussed with the class, throughout. Drama had provided the goal and the reward for the early research and writing, which otherwise might have appeared pointless and arbitrary. The setting up of specialist 'repertory' groups increased the opportunities for each child to play a meaningful part in the discussions which led to the final performances. Drama provided the fillip for getting it right: 'Would they have used that word then?' 'I don't think Joseph would be cheeky to the innkeeper, he'd be too tired.' Drama offered etymological excursions, as the children explored the ways in which the English language had lost, gained and modified words. If medieval history became more vivid in the process, that was almost a by-product, since the greater objective here was to involve every child meaningfully in the gathering and dissemination of information, and in the discussion, negotiation and collaboration which preceded the final performance.

'Accident'

Programmes of work, such as that described above, demonstrate the significance of drama in integrating many aspects of English work which might otherwise remain as disparate elements in an overcrowded timetable. Drama not only encourages those kinds of talk which might otherwise be neglected in the formal lesson, it also creates a need for many kinds of focused reading and writing. While some of this will be of the preliminary research type, much of it may form an integral part of the drama, may be written in role and will encourage the practice of less familiar registers and vocabularies.

Children are used to being warned about the dangers of running across the road or bicycling in an irresponsible manner. They are less used to analysing how accidents happen, what the consequences may be, and how perceptions of the event may differ. The drama may begin with the children listing what they would consider to be common kinds of accidents, for example:

- An old person who is rather slow in getting across the road, and perhaps rather deaf, is hit by a speeding car.
- A bicyclist fails to signal before turning right, or is simply not noticed by a car driver.
- A child follows a ball into the road, without looking first, and is hit by a car.

Groups may select different accidents or may choose to focus on the same one; they may begin by listing the personnel who will be involved in the three stages of the accident: the preface, the accident, and the aftermath. The preface will set the scene in some way, perhaps explaining the reason for the journey of at least one of those involved, even introducing an element of irony; perhaps the journey was not necessary or was undertaken against advice.

Some will want to stage the accident, though children pretending to be vehicles generally results in rather facile drama. Children can gain from learning that action does not have to be shown but can be revealed retrospectively (as in Shakespeare's *Antony and Cleopatra*) through the vivid language of a witness. The teacher may need to demonstrate the possibilities of retrospective narrative by describing a real or imagined event and asking the class to ask questions which will reveal further significant information. The aftermath might entail the improvisation of any of a number of scenes, in turn, each demonstrating different perceptions of the accident; the scene in the casualty department as parents anxiously question doctor or child; the conversation between the ambulance officer and the victim, or driver; the taking of statements by the police

149

officer called to the accident; the scene as angry mothers complain to a local journalist that an accident black spot has claimed another victim.

This could legitimately result in a wide range of relevant writing: the contents of the police officer's notebook, or ambulance officer's log book; the victim's letter, sent from hospital; the driver's formal description of the accident, for insurance purposes; the report or letter published in the local newspaper. Each will call for a different style and vocabulary; some will purport to be objective, while others are likely to be highly subjective and may try to win over the reader. There is little point in going to these lengths if children have not been challenged by the drama to use language in ways appropriate to the contexts, or if they are left confused about the different roles of the professionals involved in such incidents. The teacher will need to ensure that she at least is well-informed and may, where feasible, valuably invite representatives of these agencies into the classroom, to answer children's questions.

Simple simulation exercises

Work such as that described above often results in the identification of problems which invite resolution through simulation exercises: if an accident black spot has been identified, what is to be done? What are the possible options? Who will make or influence the decisions? If the construction of a by-pass seems the only solution, where is this to go? What are the implications of following the route favoured by the local authority? What are the alternative routes? Which pressure groups are likely to fight such a proposal? What arguments are they likely to employ? Children do not need to rely on commercially produced materials for such exercises, when they can decide the background data for themselves, perhaps mapping the area at the time of the proposal, producing role profiles for those who will become victims of the proposal, those who will have something to gain, and those who, though not directly affected, will fight for or against as representatives of local groups. Where these materials are successful, they can be attractively displayed or duplicated, providing models for the work of others.

Simulation exercises imply the taking on of realistic (though not necessarily contemporary) roles and the presentation of different arguments in order to attempt to resolve a dispute. It is sometimes tacitly assumed that they are only really suitable for pupils in the upper reaches of secondary schools, but there is no reason why primary age children, who are capable of devising quite complicated 'let's imagine' games, should not take on a particular role and argument.

> Each of you is a member of the Benjamin family. Mr and Mrs Benjamin have won the first prize in a competition, a new car worth £7,000. Mr Benjamin wants to keep the prize and sell his old car, since he has always wanted a new one. The other members of the family, Mrs Benjamin, Sandra, Darren and Gran, wish to sell the prize and use the money for other things which they feel the family needs more.
>
> Decide which member of the family you will be and write a role card, setting out your age, interests, and what you would like to spend the money on, and why. You will need to persuade the others that your idea is the best one, so think of some strong reasons to support your case.

Simulation exercises can go beyond typical small-scale domestic disputes, to explore broader contemporary issues, at times obliquely, through the creation of an imaginary world.

This junior class has been using the story of the wooden horse of Troy as a focus for drama. The period of waiting which precedes the Greek attack is explored from the viewpoints of several interested parties: King Priam and his councillors, the Greek soldiers claustrophobically imprisoned in the horse, local residents whose road is blocked by its arrival, and a quick-witted entrepreneur who plans to exploit the horse as a tourist attraction. Prior to any attempt at improvisation, the children are asked to identify the dilemmas which face these characters, for example: should the king and his councillors play a waiting game, or should they assume the worst and attempt a pre-emptive strike? How will they convince the people that the decision was a valid one if they are proved to be mistaken? When should the Greek soldiers break out of the horse to stage the attack? How will the disgruntled residents convince the local militia that the horse must be removed? What promotional tactics will reap the entrepreneur a healthy

151

profit without attracting the critical attention of the soldiers or the local people?

Once this work has been completed, the teacher exploits one pupil's assertion, 'It couldn't happen today. . . ,' to focus the class's attention on any new arrival, either today or in the future, which might cause argument, or even destroy their town. The suggestions include a new motorway, the erection of buildings on farmland or parkland, the arrival of new people, the damming of a river, creatures landing from another planet, the arrival of a strange illness. The teacher feels that several suggestions invite exploration of a contentious local issue, the provision of a permanent gypsy site, within a mile of the school, but wishes to broaden the issue to challenge pupils to consider the plight of all those who are considered abnormal or nonconformist in some way. She divides the class into two; one half will become the inhabitants (the Nurpas) and the other half the visitors (the Invas). Each side is given a relevant profile to read silently.

The Invas

You came to the planet Nurp from across the universe five years ago. At first you thought no one lived there. The land looked fertile but nothing seemed to be growing. There were no buildings and none of the wonderful inventions you take for granted. But then you met small groups of strange-looking people who refused to take their hats off to you because they said they must wear them in honour of their god Kurda. When you told these 'Nurpas' that you would take their land because they had neglected it, they became very angry, so you put them into camps and told them they would only come out when they agreed to be ruled by you, and agreed to work harder.

Now you rule the planet and the Nurpas are still living in camps, which are untidy, smelly and full of diseases that Invas never get. You are outnumbered by the Nurpas by 2 to 1. It is difficult farming the land when there are so few of you, and when so many have to guard the camps.

Group A

You want to keep the Nurpas in the camps since you feel they do not deserve to be let out. Why is this? What are your plans for the future of the planet?

Group B

You want to give the Nurpas more freedom. Why is this? What are your plans for the future of the planet?

The Nurpas

The planet Nurp is the only planet you know; you have always lived here. You have learned to make tree houses and cave homes and to plant the few crops you need in order to feed yourselves. You worship the god of the harvest, Harva, and the god of your ancestors, Kurda, who said that you should always wear a hat in her honour. While you do argue among yourselves, you have never had a war; you are too busy finding enough to eat, and anyway you do not have any weapons, apart from sticks and stones.

Your world was ruined when the aggressive Invas came. They marched through your fields and flattened the harvest. They cut down your tree houses, tried to stop you worshipping Kurda and Harva, and tried to force you to worship their god Sav, whose name you refuse to mention. When you insisted that this was your land and refused to do what they said, they forced you into prison camps and gave you only poor soil on which to grow your food. You outnumber the Invas by 2 to 1.

Group A

You hate the Invas. Although you will not attack them, and dare not be too rude to them, you will not co-operate and try to find ways of making life difficult for them. Why is this? What are your plans for your own future, and for the future of the planet?

Group B

You know that the Invas are secretly frightened of you because you outnumber them. You believe that the Nurpas must make a deal with the Invas and that each side must give a little.
Why is this? What are your plans for the future of the planet?

The teacher first checks that the profiles have been understood by the whole class. She offers to answer any further questions, whenever they may arise. The Nurpas and Invas are then divided into A and B groups, and each of the four ensuing groups is asked to decide each member's identity, and brief role description. These are noted for future reference. The teacher reintroduces herself as Jup, a Nurpa who was adopted by two Invas and who feels sympathy for both sides. She tells the class that the situation on Nurp has come to the attention of UPPO (the United Planets Peace Organization), and that Jup has been sent on a mission to bring both sides together so that a solution can be found. She will first make a fact-finding visit to each side in order to learn of their grievances and wishes.

Once identities have been established, the two sides are ready to improvise the scene as the As and Bs meet separately to plan for their meeting with Jup. They decide their grievances and demands. Jup's meetings with the assembled Invas and then the assembled Nurpas are stormy affairs as As and Bs vie with each other to convince Jup that their approach is the better one. Jup then reports these messages to the opposing side. In the following drama session Jup reminds the groups of the progress of the drama thus far by consulting her notes of the demands from both sides. She informs each side that they must meet separately (As and Bs together) to decide one or more compromises which will give both sides some of what they want. Once the compromises have been hammered out Jup brings the whole class together for the first time and asks spokespersons from both sides to describe their proposed compromises. The Invas suggest that a parliament should be set up with equal members from the Nurpa and Inva communities, where every member would be able to vote on every decision taken. They suggest that each people should be able to worship their own gods. The Nurpas and Jup consider the proposal; both commend and question the proposal. The Nurpas in their turn suggest that they should concentrate on what they are best at, the growing of crops, leaving the Invas free to exploit their talents as inventors. The Nurpas will pay for the new inventions with crops, while the Invas exchange their ideas for food. Jup has the final word as she praises aspects of both schemes, while pointing out that neither, alone, will solve the problem and that both will be needed if the troubled question of decision-making is to be resolved.

This programme of work was undertaken with children who were used to the challenge of adopting different roles and viewpoints and who were accustomed to the teacher's entry into role in order to plant new facts or ask searching questions. They were also quick to see the parallels between their own work and contemporary local and international issues. The work depended on the teacher taking on a supervisory role, while still leaving the groups sufficient scope for articulating their own opinions. The drama contained checks and balances, those provided by the teacher in role, and by the A and B device, which encouraged children to look at the diversity of opinion which can exist on the same side.

Any drama work which allows children the freedom to devise their own solutions inevitably risks the possibility that these solutions will fly in the face of the teacher's desired, humane outcome. Although unlikely, it is possible that a group of children will advocate the enslaving of the Nurpas, will suggest that the gypsies should be punished, or that those with the wrong-coloured faces should be deported. Such possibilities do not provide an excuse for refusing to face contentious issues, issues which are only too real to those children who experience them in the harsh world of life beyond school; nor do they diminish the importance of drama in allowing children opportunities to consider the alternatives to bigoted and blinkered remarks and solutions, and in giving them the confidence to articulate more enlightened responses.

To and from literature

Children almost invariably enjoy dramatizing a story they have enjoyed, and such enjoyment is not to be derided. But

155

dramatizations which lean too heavily on the skills of others deflect children from exploiting their own imaginative powers to generate and shape characters and events. The best stories, for drama's purpose, are the most enigmatic since they suggest so many fascinating possibilities, while simultaneously providing a firm basis for improvisation and elaboration. Comfortingly, they can provide a ready-made dénouement, thus freeing children to concentrate on the heart of the narrative.

> A vain and foolish ruler insists on wearing in public the new set of clothes made for him/her by a cunning tailor. The ruler only discovers that he/she has been tricked when a child dares to tell the truth.

> (A) who prides himself on his cleverness, tries to outsmart (B), but (B) sees through the trick and surprises (A) when he outsmarts him, only to be cheated by (A) in his turn.

> Once there was a girl called Vanessa. She went on holiday but she got on the wrong plane and she got lost in a strange country. She tried hard to find her real home and it took a long time.

The first of course summarizes 'The Emperor's New Clothes', while the second plot outline is a distillation from many of the Brer Rabbit and Anansi animal tales.[8] The third example is the work of a young writer who has produced a plot rather than a story. To insist that she adds to this would make little sense to the writer who might legitimately insist, 'But it's finished.' The plot needs fleshing out rather than accretions at the end. In each case drama can provide both the motivation and the medium for exploring how these three scenarios might be elaborated to produce any of a number of end-products: a complete story, perhaps intended for a class anthology; a musical, a play or a tape-slide sequence. The challenge of dramatizing these outlines creates the need to ask and answer just those questions which will expand these words on the page. Drama points the way to the differences between bare plot and shaped story and helps young writers to see the possibilities which are latent in the most simple idea.

Merely by casting themselves in the parts, children will be

stamping their own identities on the plot, signalling those qualities they associate with certain roles. They will need to ask the same questions which confront the thoughtful writer, if they are to give substance to the work: When did this happen? Where does Vanessa live? Who took her on holiday? Why and where did she get lost? Where was the wrong plane going? What did she do and feel when she realized what had happened? and so forth. Children who know of only one method of dramatizing an event, in strict chronological sequence, from the point of view of only one protagonist, can experiment with other techniques. For example, the class may be divided into groups, each of which receives the same outline, but a different set of instructions.

A young child once helped a rather frightening old person. In return, the old person promised the child three wishes. The child told his/her family who argued over how the wishes should be used. The first two wishes were wasted on silly or dangerous things. Annoyed by this, the child used the final wish generously, and was praised by the old person, who gave the child a suitable reward.

Instruction 1 Act out the story from the point of view of the child, so make it clear that he or she is the leading person by having him or her on stage as much as possible.

          2 Act out the story from the point of view of the old person, so make it clear that he or she is the leading person by showing what his or her life is like before the child comes, and by having him or her on stage as much as possible.

          3 Act out the story from the point of view of the child and family. Do not cast anybody as the old person.

          4 Imagine that all this happened seventy years ago. Act out the scene as the child, now a great-grandparent, tells his great-grandchildren this story, answers their questions, and hears about their dealings with old people.

> 5 Imagine that the old person has a great secret
>   which he or she only tells the child near the
>   end of your play.

The outline and sets of instructions are read through and discussed by the whole class, prior to the formation of groups. The teacher asks the children to suggest key words in the outline which suggest openings for drama. She gives them an example, 'frightening': who has the old person frightened? How? Is he or she really frightening, or just misunderstood? The class suggests others, 'helped', 'argued', 'wasted', 'generously' and 'rewarded'. The children are encouraged to suggest strategies which may help to fulfil the instructions; the third of these puzzles some until they grasp that reporting techniques can recreate an event not actually shown. Discussion also focuses on where the acting out might begin, disclosing the opportunity to start the action well before the first meeting of child and old person.

Although the whole class has discussed all the instructions, each group is unaware of the instructions received by other groups, thus giving the final performances an added spice as the audience is asked to deduce the relevant instruction from the style of the interpretation. After each performance actors and audience identify and consider the techniques which have been used and relate these to possible ways of writing up the performances, in prose or script form.

This ability to see dramatic possibilities, to stretch, interpolate and elaborate, is a prerequisite for building documentary drama. Children who wish to dramatize an Edwardian diary, the coming of the railway to their community, a local mining accident, or a visit from Queen Victoria, will have access to the bare facts, but will need to make the imaginative leap to clothe these with the convincing substance of domestic and social life. They will need to cut a path into the drama: how will the events unfold? Through the experiences of an individual, a group, or more than one group? Will a narrator be needed, or music? Will songs be used to provide light relief, to reinforce the events, or to reveal characters' feelings? Children will need to draw out the highs and lows, the moments of conflict, stress, danger, relief and joy which provide the switchback momentum which sustains what otherwise might seem a slight event.

Drama offers a valuable medium for answering those 'What do you think will happen next . . . and why?' questions which constructively accompany story telling and reading. Children's attention is likely to be more firmly fixed on a story if they know that the teller may stop at any moment and challenge the audience to devise an appropriate ending through discussion or drama. These solutions may be shared with the rest of the class and each group may be questioned about the rationale for their chosen answer, or answers. Ideally, in answering these questions children will demonstrate their understanding of the story and their insight into characterization: 'At the beginning of the story it said that she was really looking forward to the picnic, so. . . ,' 'Because he wouldn't steal from someone he was so frightened of, who could catch him so easily. . . .' The class's solutions can be compared with that provided by the original author, whether adult or child. Drama can also come to the aid of the child who has written a satisfying beginning and middle to his work but is at a loss for a suitable ending. The challenge may be taken up by a group which tries out possible solutions for size.

'A way in'

Teachers who come new to drama may find that their problem is less one of 'What shall we do?' but more one of 'How shall we do it?'; that is ideas may be plentiful but organizational strategies for using them may be less apparent. Understandably, these concerns often relate to the perceived constraints which frequently seem to accompany drama: 'I can only spare an hour a week. . . ,' 'If we're going to do any it's got to be in the classroom most of the time, because the hall will be used for gym and orchestra,' 'If we want the hall it'll have to be after swimming, and they're so excitable then. . . ,' 'I want to do something that's not too ambitious the first time so that I feel in control. . . .' These are all comments made by class teachers who would like to take the plunge but who, in the words of one, 'need to find a way in'. Of course there is no prescribed recipe for a first drama session, merely a few common sense principles which together provide a framework for the work.

159

1 Constraints such as those indicated above, rather than insuperable problems, are factors which at best can be exploited, and at worst can helpfully indicate the direction the drama might take.

2 The first session will inevitably signal to the children the teacher's view of what drama is all about. The work in the first session, however modest, should thus be constructive and enjoyable, controlled but creative.

3 The teacher should feel particularly secure in her role in this first session and thus is unlikely to want to delegate a great deal of responsibility for the course of the work to pupils. Thus she may avoid strenuous 'Captain's Coming' kinds of games which may over-excite children, in favour of more sedentary and concentrated activities which form a bridge between conventional classroom activities and the novel conventions of drama.

4 Each child, while being stimulated by the work in this first session, should not feel put at risk by potentially embarrassing or over-demanding tasks. He too should feel safe and should taste early success.

5 The work should not invite too many deviant activities which then have to be noticed and punished. Thus the space within which the work is to take place may be deliberately circumscribed and the teacher may avoid sending over-large groups of children out of her range.

The first session may introduce the theme for a programme of work, or may stand alone. Some teachers choose to concentrate on dialogue exercises in the first of early sessions, of the 'Pretend you're walking through mud...,' 'have a conversation without using the words "yes" or "no" ...' type. While children enjoy these, and learn something about control, concentration and tone from them, they are no more than exercises, warm-up preliminaries, and should not be allowed to deflect attention away from the kind of role play which allows children to bed their work in a meaningful context. Perhaps such exercises are popular because, by asking children to work alone or in pairs, they may minimize any control problems implied by group work. Of course the child who is intent on misbehaviour will find opportunities for this even when supposedly working alone, and group work should not suggest a rather flabby, 'You have ten minutes to go away and work out a story about robbers,' which may well invite facile drama and misbehaviour.

Where the teacher wishes, or where the circumstances demand it, group work may be carefully structured, perhaps through the use of a written assignment which makes some of the decisions for the children, while allowing them scope for creativity. A simple simulation profile, or a 'drama cloze' narrative, may provide such a structure and simultaneously help all the children to find some success in the first session. The drama cloze option, like all cloze work, invites children to fill the gaps in the story or poem through discussing possible insertions and relating these to the demands of the context. The piece selected can come from a story book, anthology or child's work, or, as here, may be tailor-made by the teacher, in this case for a class which has been exploring the theme 'Persuasion'.

'Persuasion'

Lesley Jones got up one morning, drew the bedroom curtains and discovered that the world outside had changed in the night. She (or he) got dressed quickly and opened the front door. Outside stood a stranger who greeted Lesley in a most peculiar way, and said that his name was Free. He explained that Lesley was now on the Planet Z and that Lesley would have to persuade someone to go with her if she was ever to return to earth.

Lesley tried to persuade Free to come with her by offering him all the money in her pocket. But Free looked angry and refused the money and said,

'I won't go with you to earth because...................................
.... '

The next person Lesley met said her name was .... She looked very friendly and merry. Lesley said, 'If you come with me to earth I'll ....
.... '

'No,' said .... 'I won't come with you because ......
.... '

The next person Lesley met looked very frightened and timid. She whispered that her name was .... Lesley looked very fierce and marched up to .... and said, 'If

you don't come with me to earth I'll ....,
....
But .... whispered, 'I'm afraid I won't come with you
because ....,
....

Lesley was feeling very cold and hungry, so she sat down
beside a bush to eat the only food she had, a bar of
chocolate. Suddenly an old person, who looked very poor
and unhappy, came from behind the bush. Lesley looked
curiously at the stranger and thought hard. She wanted her
chocolate very much but she thought that the old person
needed it even more. The old person took the chocolate
gratefully.

Next Lesley noticed that the old person was shivering so
she offered him her woolly jumper. The old person took it
and put it on and told Lesley that his name was ....
Suddenly Lesley noticed how happy the stranger looked, now
he seemed warm and well-fed and somehow younger.

'You want to go to earth don't you?' said ....
'Oh yes!' said Lesley, 'But I can't persuade anyone to come
with me.'

'Why do you think that is?' said ....
'I'm not sure,' said Lesley, 'perhaps it's because ....,
....
'How strange,' said the old person, 'for I will come with
you to earth because ....,
....

The next thing Lesley knew, the stranger had gone and she
was turning faster and faster. When she stopped she found
herself back in her little bedroom. Out of the window she
could see the earth she knew so well.

'Perhaps it was all a dream,' said Lesley. But when she
glanced at her clothes she found that her jumper had gone,
and when she searched in her pockets for the bar of
chocolate that had vanished too. But where was .... ?
After all, he had promised to come too. And then Lesley
noticed a new picture hanging above her bed. It was a
photograph of the mysterious old person, looking much
younger, and grinning from ear to ear.

'So you did come too,' said Lesley. And as if to reply the
face chuckled and gave Lesley a great friendly wink.

The teacher first reads the story through in the classroom, as expressively as possible, and discusses its content with the class. She asks the children to suggest a possible convincing insertion for the first gap. The various suggestions are considered, allowing the teacher the opportunity to stress that the children may need to experiment with several solutions before finding the best possible one. The children spend the remainder of the time in the classroom, devising and discussing answers, before moving to the hall. Here, the class is divided into groups: while one or more of them are reading out the story line, the rest will mime the parts. The teacher emphasizes that the mime will have to pay particular attention to showing the characters' feelings, and reinforces this by miming part of the story and asking the children to identify the relevant part and to describe precisely what they have seen.

In what remains of the drama session, the children work on their interpretations, dovetailing readings with action. The teacher gives help where necessary, sometimes challenging children's assumptions or injecting questions which invite children to look at their work a little more objectively. In the subsequent session different interpretations are compared. The teacher had intended to ask the children to proceed to act out the entire narrative, without narrators, but felt that this would be unnecessarily restricting, particularly given the children's eagerness to develop their own 'persuasion' ideas, through drama.

'Teeth'

Having a specific goal and audience in mind may in itself help to stimulate and structure a first drama session. In this case, the teacher tells the class that, following their work on 'Teeth', she wants to see if they are capable of teaching the infants about the importance of healthy teeth and gums, by dramatizing the 'Life Story of a Tooth' for them. The class responds to the challenge enthusiastically, and gathers around the teacher to hear her own version of this story.

The Life Story of a Tooth

This is the story of one grown-up *Tooth*. He or she belonged to a member of class ____. He was cosily asleep in his warm little gum home when one day he realized that the time had come to burst out and meet the outside world, in his owner's mouth. He was very happy with the other grown-up teeth until he discovered that a stranger had joined him, a stranger with an odd name, who kept creeping up on him when he wasn't looking. This was *Plaque*, a rather sticky, sickly, germy fellow.

Tooth noticed that Plaque would go away when his owner used *Toothbrush* and *Toothpaste*, but since this hardly ever happened, Plaque seemed to hang around more and more, with a horrible greedy grin on his face. This wasn't too bad until Tooth's owner began to eat lots of *Sweet Things*, like sweets and cakes and sugary drinks, but then Plaque looked very happy indeed and started to suck up all the sugar and changed it into *Acid*, a nasty spiteful creature who had a frightening laugh. Acid attacked poor Tooth and gave him the most terrible pain and made him wobbly on his legs. The more Tooth's owner ate Sweet Things and didn't clean his teeth, the worse the pain got until Acid, with that dreadful laugh of his, knocked a hole in Tooth's head. Tooth tried to scream out to his owner, but could make no sound. Gradually though the pain got the message across, and Tooth found himself taken to *Dentist*. 'Oh no,' thought Tooth, 'this is the end. If Dentist can't help me, I'm done for.'

Dentist took one look at Tooth and shook her head, 'You haven't been brushing this Tooth, have you?' she asked Tooth's owner. 'This Tooth must have been shiny and healthy once but now look at him, knocked about, in pain and black and blue. I don't know if I can save him; it's touch and go, you may have come here just in time.'

Fortunately Dentist was very clever and kind and knew how to patch up a seriously ill Tooth. She stopped the pain, cleaned out and filled in the great black hole, and asked to be introduced to Toothbrush.

'Nothing wrong with Toothbrush,' said Dentist, 'She's young and bristly and will look after Tooth, but only if she's used twice a day, after breakfast and last thing at night. And remember, not so many Sweet Things, try fresh fruit and savoury things instead.'

Tooth breathed a great sigh of relief, particularly when he discovered that Dentist had really scared his owner, who didn't want a mouth full of very expensive false teeth. The story ended happily, for Tooth expects to live for another seventy years at least.

The teacher reads her version a second time and asks for volunteers to play the characters. The children are divided into groups; each is given a cast list, for completion.

Cast

. . . .	Tooth
. . . .	Plaque
. . . .	Toothbrush
. . . .	Toothpaste
. . . .	Sweet Things
. . . .	Acid
. . . .	Dentist

Fill in the names you have chosen, for example:

       Lady   Lavinia   Sweet Things

The groups are asked to devise and tell their own story, entitled 'The Life Story of a Tooth', involving the characters in the cast list, and any others they may think are appropriate. The story will, like the teacher's, form the framework for mime and, where the group wish, for dialogue. The narrator device gives a backbone to the work of these children who come new to drama, and focuses attention on the shaping of the story. There is little danger that the groups will slavishly imitate the teacher's story since they never have access to a copy, though they can consult the teacher in order to verify the facts. The teacher's model is exploited for just long enough to suggest how drama and narrative may vividly combine to convey a message, and one which will reach a wider audience of younger children, or adults.

The teacher in role

There is, happily, no set progression in drama which determines what should be done, when and with which age groups. There is certainly no need to defer attempting dialogue or improvisation until children are confident movers and mimers, since mime is not necessarily easier than improvisations which include dialogue, and children may become inhibited improvisers if drama is over-dissected and fragmented. Nor need we wait before adopting a role other than that of teacher. Children are usually only too ready to enter into a new imaginative world once the teacher says, 'When I speak to you I shall be speaking as someone else . . .' or 'When I stand up I shall be the wise man on the hill so please treat me with respect,' and will readily respond to reminders that, 'When I come round to visit you I may not be myself, so listen carefully.'

There are good reasons for beginning the first session with the entry of the teacher in an unfamiliar role, without warning. After the initial insuck of breath and momentary disorientation, children almost invariably enter into the novelty of the occasion, responding appropriately. Rather than informing the class, 'Today we are going to see how good you are at asking sensible questions to find out information,' the teacher may enter in role as a person from past, present, or future, adopting a suitable accent, mannerisms and movements and inviting questions: '. . . and I am here today because I have heard you wish to know what life was like for a maidservant in a country house one hundred years ago. . . .' Of course the teacher should not monopolize the delights of role play, tempting though this is; she is there to suggest one possible model, to invite thoughtful questions and therefore careful listening, and to challenge pupils to enter similarly wholeheartedly into role play. Once children have questioned their visitor, and perhaps detected any flaws in his answers (for such detective work helps to focus attention), children can themselves adopt and develop imaginary characters. These can be fleshed out with the help of questionnaires devised with a colleague, and through imaginary studio interviews. At this point, space allowing, children can demonstrate their characters in action, showing perhaps how they get dressed, eat their favourite food or perform a domestic task. This may lead into a short mimed sequence, perhaps recreating the circumstances in which two of the characters first met.

A similar role play device may initiate an exploration of the kinds of persuasive tactics employed in selling or advertising: the teacher enters in role as an old-fashioned market trader who uses sales patter to promote his or her goods, and in so doing creates a world of imaginary customers around the stall. Coming out of role, the teacher asks the class to identify the persuasive devices which the trader used, and to suggest others that he might have employed. The class is invited to 'see what happens when the trader tries to sell a more fantastic product'. They are warned that this time they must be prepared to take a more active part, and must also be ready to ask the teacher searching questions about the product at the end.

The trader tries to sell his customers a pet rock, stressing, among other qualities, its docile manner, cheap upkeep, loyal nature and celebrity status ('as seen in Hollywood . . .'). He produces several sizes of pets, relating each to a potential buyer in the audience. Once the class has thoroughly interrogated the trader, in some cases moving spontaneously into role, the teacher asks them, working with a neighbour, to list any products (other than food) which they might expect to see on sale in a local market. Once the suggestions have been shared, the teacher broadens the inquiry to include goods which they might expect to find in markets in other countries.

In pairs, children choose any one real product from their lists and decide what their selling lines will be. These are used as the basis for a demonstration of how they would attempt to sell this from their stall. The process is repeated as each pair attempts to sell a fantastic new product. The concluding discussion focuses on the work children have seen: which of the products might they choose to buy? Why? What questions would they wish to ask these traders? Such work might lead logically to an exploration of the ways in which similar persuasive tactics are used in the marketing and advertising of a new product, from the selection of its name and image, through to the selection of the advertising media, and the editing of the advertisement. While this may sound more suited to pupils in the third or fourth years of secondary schooling, junior age children at least rise to the challenge of making and justifying the decisions involved in image-building of this sort. They will find the task more interesting and meaningful once they know a little more of the part played by advertising agencies, and having analysed the apparent rationale behind product names and images.

'Bazania'

Entry into role provides the teacher with opportunities to direct children's work from within the drama; it helps to dissolve some, though inevitably not all, of the inhibitions which accompany the roles and relationships of pupil and teacher. If the role is a provocative one, as in the example which follows, even the more introverted children may be startled into forthright responses.

The teacher enters in role, wearing a vivid mask (or head-dress) as Baza, ruler of Bazania, the most distant planet in the solar system, and greets the class as Bazanian citizens. Since, as they know, all Bazanians are duty bound to have single names which end with the letter 'a', she asks the citizens to state their names in turn. Baza strides up and down in a forbidding manner as she informs her people that, following a trip to Durro, a neighbouring planet, she has decided to ban all money. Henceforth barter will be used. In role, the concept of barter is explored.

Baza describes the wonderful products she has seen on Durro, foot baths which induce happiness, nightingales which can be programmed to sing selected songs and many more. She recounts the amazing skills she discovered there, including a boy who always knows where to dig for precious objects, and a woman who can understand all the gestures of animals.

The Bazanians are paired; one will be the seller of a wonderful product, while the other will be the possessor of a remarkable skill. Any spare pupil will become an Elder, or a Quality Tester. The citizens are informed that only those who have an unusual product or skill to offer will be permitted to remain on Baza. In pairs, the Bazanians demonstrate their offerings to each other in a barter scene. Baza circulates, being dictatorial or encouraging, as she considers appropriate. She asks her Quality Tester to recommend those whose offerings should be seen, since they seem promising. All the citizens are warned that, should they falter in their demonstrations, they face any of a number of typically devious Bazanian punishments; walking along a spider's web without falling off or smiling, for a trival offence, or being dessicated in the royal kitchens, for a serious crime against Baza. However, a suitable Bazanian reward, of the recipient's choice, will be given to those whose offerings are most impressive.

Since all those seen pass the test, Baza commends her people on their cleverness, but warns them that because of this success their next task will be more difficult. They are asked to devise a test which will ensure that Baza's daughter, Marzipana, finds a suitable husband; he must be kind, honest, and brave. The Bazanians report back to Baza with their tests. She next challenges them to produce their own cunning tests which might be used to challenge any two Bazanians. She gives the following as an example; two Bazanians are to build an invisible sculpture, which is yet visible to the audience and which is bigger than the sculptors, who must then tell an interesting tale associated with their work.

The Bazanians' imaginative and descriptive skills are thoroughly tested as they devise their ingenious challenges: two Bazanians must have a conversation in their native language, in which every word ends in an 'a'; two more must demonstrate how to cook the Bazanian national dish, on board a spaceboat. Once the tests have been passed by the most punctilious Baza, her citizens are allowed to nominate another pair of citizens to carry out the test. This is performed ritualistically, as each couple approach their targets with their own unique Bazanian nominating gestures. Baza draws her people together to commend their work and to regret the fact that she has not, as yet, been able to whittle down their number. She promises harder challenges to come. The class is dismissed, still in role.

The subsequent session begins with Baza in irascible mood, complaining about the lacklustre national newspaper, *The Bazanian Stara*. She has therefore not only imprisoned the journalists, but has sentenced them to write every complimentary adjective they can think of, to describe their leader, on their cell walls. Turning to the citizens, she bellows, 'Let us show these nincompoops, these lazy, good-for-nothing journalists, how many ways Baza can be praised.' The citizens respond with a long list of appropriate adjectives (only later will the teacher ask the class for more accurate ways of describing Baza).

Baza informs the citizens that the best of their number will be appointed as journalists, but they must first prove their worth. They will be sent, in pairs, to new planets. The pair who return with the most vivid tales of the amazing things they have seen will have the chance to publish their accounts (with the aid of the Bazanian computer) and will earn the right to test Baza in some way. A few accounts are heard, and the tellers are quizzed by their audience. Baza decides that until she has read all the accounts she will be in no position to select the best; she thus decrees that all tales must be written down and accompanied by maps, diagrams or illustrations, where appropriate.

Once this work is complete, the teacher divests herself of power by inciting a coup. She passes a note to a pupil, prior to the drama session:

> *Please do not show this to anyone else*
>
> At the beginning of our drama lesson Baza will call her
> people 'idiots'. After she has used this word please call out to
> her loudly:
> You might say:
> How dare you call us idiots? It's time we ruled ourselves.
> What do you say, Bazanians?
> Or, you might make up your own speech which calls on your
> people to find another ruler.
> Even if Baza tells you off for saying this, *insist* that you are
> right and she must go.

When the pupil chosen objects in this way, Baza is initially speechless, then blustering, and finally cringing. She offers to help the citizens to decide the best alternative to her tyranny and does so by becoming a scribe, as suggestions are made. She plants questions which encourage the Bazanians to anticipate the implications of certain options: 'But if we have a new ruler how can we guarantee that the mistakes of the past are not made again?' On occasions, she challenges the class to think again by gleefully accepting proposals wholeheartedly: 'What a wonderful idea, we'll do without a ruler, and then no one will need to make a decision about anything, will they?'

Eventually, the Bazanians decide on regional councils, thus

enabling the teacher, in a subsequent session, to challenge these with a problem: two of the councils are at loggerheads over the siting of a new spaceboat station. This quarrel threatens war and thus all the other councils are faced with the task of helping the two antagonists to come to a peaceful solution.

In the course of these sessions, the children had been challenged to think quickly and imaginatively, to collaborate and negotiate and to listen carefully. Their oral and written story telling skills were tested, as were their powers to present, sustain, and detect the flaws in arguments. The teacher hoped that they had also learned that bullies can be deflated by opponents who stand their ground and argue their case, and that talking problems through can resolve conflict. Clearly the world of Bazania could be used to explore other issues, discrimination, favouritism, the needs of the elderly or the young, vandalism; and other areas of learning: map-making, the documentation of history, dictionary work, model-making. Provided the programme is not over-extended, children respond enthusiastically to such themes, sometimes refusing to let go of their Bazanian identities at the end of the sessions.

'Bazania' is one modest example of the integrating and focusing power of dramatic role play which, in freeing children from sometimes rigid classroom roles, invites new relationships and registers. As one child recently commented in her personal journal,

> I like drama. You can be all sorts of people not just yourself and it's all right if you have problems because you can sort them out and learn things and have fun and then still be you at the end.

References

Chapter 1 English and the primary school curriculum

1 *Report of the Consultative Committee on the Primary School* (The Hadow Report), London, HMSO, 1931.
2 Report of the Central Advisory Council for Education (England), *Children and their Primary Schools* (The Plowden Report), London, HMSO, 1967.
3 *Report of the Consultative Committee on Infant and Nursery Schools* (The Hadow Report), London, HMSO, 1933.
4 M. Galton, B. Simon and P. Croll, *Inside the Primary Classroom* (report of the ORACLE project), London, Routledge & Kegan Paul, 1980, p.43.
5 The Plowden Report, op. cit., p.461.
6 Ibid., p.19.
7 Ibid., p.19.
8 Ibid., p.25.
9 Ibid., p.187.
10 Ibid., p.201.
11 Ibid., p.7.
12 Ibid., p.194.
13 Ibid., p.201.
14 See J. Barker Lunn, NFER, 'Junior School Teachers: their methods and practices', in *Educational Research*, vol.26, no.3, 1984.
15 Department of Education and Science, *Primary Education in England: A Survey by HM Inspectors of Schools*, London, HMSO, 1978. Department of Education and Science, *Education 5 to 9: An Illustrative Survey of 80 First Schools in England*, London, HMSO, 1982.
16 Schools Council, *Primary Practice: A Sequel to 'the Practical Curriculum'*, Schools Council Working Paper 75, London, Methuen Educational, 1983, pp.16–17.

17 R. Alexander, *Primary Teaching*, London, Holt, Rinehart & Winston, 1984.

18 The Plowden Report, op. cit., p.188.

19 J. Dean, *Organizing Learning in the Primary School Classroom*, London, Croom Helm, 1983.

20 See P. Ashton, P. Kneen and F. Davies, *Aims into Practice in the Primary Classroom*, London, University of London Press, 1975, chapter 6, 'Aims into practice: teachers' reviews'.

21 For those coming new to such an inquiry, the following texts offer accessible starting points: J. Britton, *Language and Learning*, London, Penguin Books, 1970; A. Wilkinson, *The Foundations of Language*, London, Oxford University Press, 1971; A. Wilkinson, *Language and Education*, London, Oxford University Press, 1975.

Chapter 2   Reading for meaning

1 Department of Education and Science, *Primary Education in England: A Survey by HM Inspectors of Schools*, London, HMSO, 1978.

2 Ibid., p.47.

3 Ibid., p.47.

4 Ibid., p.52.

5 Ibid., p.48.

6 V. Southgate, H. Arnold and S. Johnson, *Extending Beginning Reading*, London, Heinemann Educational Books, 1981.

7 Ibid., p.120.

8 Ibid., p.126: thus reinforcing Michael Bassey's findings, in *Nine Hundred Primary School Teachers*, London, NFER, 1978, p.75, that at least 75 per cent of the teachers of infants in his sample expected their pupils to read aloud to an adult on not fewer than three days in every five.

9 Southgate *et al.*, op. cit., p.147.

10 Ibid., p.142.

11 Ibid., p.146.

12 Ibid., p.261.

13 Department of Education and Science, *Education 5 to 9: An Illustrative Survey of 80 First Schools in England*, London, HMSO, 1982.

14 Ibid., p.5.

15 Ibid., p.5.

16 Ibid., p.5.

17 Ibid., p.7.

18 Ibid., p.8.

19   Department of Education and Science, *A Language for Life* (The Bullock Report), London, HMSO, 1975, p.127.

20   Helen Arnold, in *Listening to Children Reading*, London, Hodder & Stoughton, 1982, pp.26–7, presents a salutary reminder of how the text may appear to the inexperienced reader. See also V. Edwards and S. Sheldon, 'The Experience of Reading', in P534 Course Team, *Every Child's Language*, Book 1, Open University INSET, London, Open University, 1985, p.45.

21   See 'flap' books, for example, the Spot books by Eric Hill, Heinemann, from *Where's Spot?* to *Spot Goes to School*; and the more enlightened and less gruesome of the very popular 'game' books which invite readers to decide the outcome themselves, for example, Cambridge University Press's 'Storytrails' series.

22   A. Cameron, *The Julian Stories*, London, Gollancz, 1982, and Armada, 1984.

23   See, for example, M. Hoffman, 'Choosing children's books' in M. Hoffman, R. Jeffcoate, J. Maybin and N. Mercer, *Children, Language and Literature*, P530 CB, Open University INSET, London, Open University Press, 1982; S. Dale, S. Gerrard, M. Hoffman, *Finding Out About Children's Books: An Information Guide for Teachers*, P530 IG, Open University INSET, London, Open University Press, 1982; J. Elkin and P. Triggs (eds), *The Books for Keeps Guide to Children's Books for a Multi-cultural Society*, 2 vols, for age ranges 0–7, 8–12, London, Books for Keeps, 1985; A. Raddan, *Exploring Cultural Diversity, An Annotated Fiction List*, London, School Library Association, 1985; N. Chambers (ed.), *The Signal Selection of Children's Books*, London, Thimble Press (annual survey); J. Bennett, *Learning to Read with Picture Books*, a Signal Bookguide, 3rd edn, London, Thimble Press, 1985.

24   For further information concerning the involvement of parents in teaching children to read, see P. Hannon, R. Long, J. Weinburger and L. Whitehurst, *Involving Parents in the Teaching of Reading*, Occasional Paper no.3, Division of Education, University of Sheffield, 1985, (an annotated bibliography); J. Trelease, *The Read Aloud Hand-Book*, London, Penguin, 1984.

25   For examples of the involvement of parents in classroom reading development see D. Houlton, *All Our Languages, A Handbook for the Multilingual Classroom*, London, Edward Arnold, 1985, chapter 3 in particular.

26   See M. McKenzie, *Learning to Read and Reading*, ILEA Curriculum Guideline, London, 1979, for a fascinating glimpse of how 5-year-old Barbara's understanding of a fairy story becomes increasingly more accurately reconciled to the reality of the text.

27   See Southgate *et al.*, op. cit., and E. Lunzer and K. Gardner (eds),

The Effective Use of Reading, London, Heinemann Educational Books, 1979.

28 See J. Maybin (ed.), 'Whole-school reading periods', in Hoffman *et al.*, op. cit., p.121, for an example of USSR in practice in a primary school.

29 See Arnold, op. cit., chapter 4, 'Miscue analysis in the classroom', which adapts Kenneth Goodman's work on miscue analysis for use in the primary classroom. (See also K. Goodman, 'Analysis of oral reading miscues: applied psycholinguistics', *Reading Research Quarterly*, vol. 1, no.3.)

30 Report of the Central Advisory Council for Education (England), *Children and their Primary Schools* (The Plowden Report), volume 1: Report, London, HMSO, 1967, p.215.

31 The Bullock Report, op. cit., p.xxxi.

32 Ibid., p.109.

33 D. Mackay, B. Thompson and P. Schaub, *Breakthrough to Literacy Teachers' Manual*, London, Longman for the Schools Council, 2nd edn, 1979, p.3.

34 *Primary Education in England: A Survey by HM Inspectors of Schools*, op. cit., p.47.

35 Ginn Reading 360, *Levels 1 and 2 Teachers' Resource Book*, London, Ginn & Co., 2nd edn, 1982, p.1.

36 The Bullock Report, op. cit., p.115.

37 Southgate *et al.*, op. cit., p.120.

38 Ibid., p.122.

39 J. Bennett, 'Learning to read with real books', in Hoffman *et al.*, op. cit., p.14.

40 S. Bates, 'A good read, a "real books" policy', *Times Educational Supplement*, 8 November 1985, p.47.

41 L. Waterland, *Read With Me, An Apprenticeship Approach to Reading*, London, Thimble Press, 1985.

42 Ibid., p.13–14.

43 Ibid., p.32.

Chapter 3   Writing: processes and purposes

1 T. Gorman, J. White, M. Hargreaves, M. Maclure and A. Tate, *Language Performance in Schools, 1982 Primary Survey Report*, Assessment of Performance Unit, London, DES, 1984, p.172.

2 School Curriculum Development Committee, *About Writing* (pamphlet), London, 1986, p.2.

3 J. Tamburrini, J. Willig and C. Butler, 'Children's conceptions of writing', in *The Development of Children's Imaginative Writing*, H. Cowie (ed.), London, Croom Helm, 1984.

4   Ibid., p.197.

5   Ibid., p.199.

6   F. Smith, *Writing and the Writer*, London, Heinemann
    Educational Books, 1982.

7   Ibid., p.130.

8   Department of Education and Science, *Primary Education in
    England: A Survey by HM Inspectors of Schools*, London,
    HMSO, 1978, p.48.

9   N. Martin, P. D'Arcy, B. Newton and R. Parker, *Writing and
    Learning Across the Curriculum 11–16* (Schools Council project
    report), London, Ward Lock Educational, 1976, p.15.

10 Ibid., p.17.

11 This was one of the more significant findings from the ORACLE
    project, reported in M. Galton, B. Simon and P. Croll, *Inside the
    Primary Classroom*, London, Routledge & Kegan Paul, 1980.

12 D. Crystal, *Linguistics*, London, Penguin, 1971, p.20.

13 See, for example, P. Smith and A. Inglis, *New Nelson
    Handwriting, Teacher's Manual*, London, Nelson, 1984; R.
    Sassoon, *The Practical Guide to Children's Handwriting*,
    London, Thames & Hudson, 1983.

14 *Primary Education in England*, op. cit., p.50.

15 M. Armstrong, *Closely Observed Children, The Diary of a
    Primary Classroom*, London, Writers and Readers in association
    with Chameleon, 1980, p.18.

Chapter 4   Routes into writing

1   'Little Red Riding Hood' is one of many stories with a fascinating
    international pedigree. The ILEA English Centre team's *Changing
    Stories*, London, ILEA English Centre, 1984, brings together
    versions of the 'Red Riding Hood' story in order to demonstrate
    the ways in which historical context and changing audiences
    decide the interpretation of the tale. *Changing Stories* and its
    companion volume, *Making Stories*, published by the same team,
    also 1984, are both highly recommended to those who are
    interested in exploring (with older pupils) the ways in which
    shared plots have been elaborated by different ages and cultures,
    and the assumptions and conventions which underpin traditional
    tales.

Chapter 5   A place for poetry

1   Department of Education and Science, *A Language for Life*

(The Bullock Report), London, HMSO, 1975, p.135.

2   Department of Education and Science, *Primary Education in England: A Survey by HM Inspectors of Schools*, London, HMSO, 1978, p.47.

3   K. Calthrop and J. Ede (eds), *Not 'Daffodils' Again! Teaching Poetry 9–13*, Schools Council Programme 2, London, Longman, 1984.

4   Ibid., p.1.

5   T. Gorman, J. White, M. Hargreaves, M. Maclure and A. Tate, *Language Performance in Schools, 1982 Primary Survey Report*, Assessment of Performance Unit, London, DES, 1984, p.157.

6   Ibid., p.175.

7   J. Tamburrini, J. Willig, C. Butler, 'Children's conceptions of writing', in *The Development of Children's Imaginative Writing*, J. Cowie (ed.), London, Croom Helm, 1984.

8   T. Gorman *et al.*, op. cit.

9   Ibid., p.175.

10 K. Webb (ed.), *I Like This Poem*, London, Penguin (Puffin), 1979.

11 T. Hughes, *Poetry in the Making*, London, Faber & Faber, 1967, p.18.

12 See, for example, Catherine Storr's 'Monday's Child' in *Poetry 1, The First Lick of the Lolly*, Moira Andrew (ed.), London, Macmillan Education, 1986, p.71; Michael Rosen's 'I Went to the Doctor' and 'The Train now Standing', in *Wouldn't You Like To Know*, Michael Rosen, London, Penguin (Puffin), 1981, pp.59 and 51 respectively; Gyles Brandreth's supremely short 'Ode to a Goldfish' in *A Second Poetry Book*, J. Foster (ed.), London, Oxford University Press, 1980, p.75.

13 See, for example, Robert D. Hoeft's 'If Things Grew Down' in *Poetry 1, The First Lick of the Lolly*, Moira Andrew (ed.), op. cit., p.121; Russell Hoban's 'The Friendly Cinnamon Bun' in *All Sorts of Poems*, Ann Thwaite (ed.), London, Methuen (Magnet), 1978, p.88 (see also David Hornsby's 'Tom's Bomb' and Jacqueline Segal's 'A Blink', in the same anthology, pp.101 and 113 respectively); Roger McGough's 'Gruesome' in *You Tell Me*, Roger McGough and Michael Rosen, London, Penguin (Puffin), 1979, p.48.

14 See, for example, Gareth Owen's 'Boredom' and Edwin Morgan's 'Spacepoem 3: Off Course' in *Writing Poems*, M. Harrison and C. Stuart-Clark, London, Oxford University Press, pp.58 and 104 respectively; Peter Young's 'Hands' in *A First Poetry Book*, J. Foster (ed.), London, Oxford University Press, 1979, p.9; John C. Head's 'Monday Morning' in *Poetry 1, The First Lick of the Lolly*, Moira Andrew (ed.), op. cit., p.70.

References

15 Maggie Cook, writing in the *Guardian*, 3 November 1984.

16 J. Nicholls, 'Breakfast for One' in *Poetry 1, The First Lick of the Lolly*, Moira Andrew (ed.), op. cit., p.112.

17 See the excellent *Word Games* and *More Word Games*, both edited by Sandy Brownjohn and Janet Whitaker, London, Hodder & Stoughton, both 1985.

18 See, for example, S. Brownjohn and J. Whitaker, *More Word Games*, op. cit., pp.12–20, and M. Harrison and C. Stuart-Clark, *Writing Poems*, op. cit., pp.56–7, 59–61.

19 M. Rosen, *Wouldn't You Like To Know*, op. cit., p.35.

20 Ibid., p.46.

21 Found in *All Sorts of Poems*, A. Thwaite (ed.), op. cit., p.14.

22 Ibid., p.70.

23 Ibid., p.109.

24 Found in *Speaking To You*, Michael Rosen and David Jackson (eds), London, Macmillan Education, 1984, p.85.

25 Ibid., p.118.

26 Found in *I Like That Stuff*, Morag Styles (ed.), Cambridge, Cambridge University Press, 1984, p.56.

27 Found in *African Poetry for Schools*, Book 1, Noel Machin (ed.), London, Longman, 1978, p.21.

28 Dorothy Clancy and David Gill, *One Potato, Two Potato*, London, Macmillan Education, 1985.

29 In writing this chapter I have deliberately limited my selection of poems to those found in a few, highly recommended, anthologies. These are *A First, Second, Third, Fourth, Poetry Book*, all edited by John Foster, London, Oxford University Press, 1979, 1980, 1982, 1982, respectively; *A First Lick of the Lolly*, Moira Andrew (ed.), London, Macmillan Education, 1986 (the first in a series of four poetry anthologies); *I Like That Stuff*, Morag Styles (ed.), London, Cambridge University Press, 1984; *Speaking to You*, Michael Rosen and David Jackson (eds), London, Macmillan Education, London, 1984; *Wouldn't You Like To Know*, Michael Rosen, London, Penguin (Puffin), 1981; *You Tell Me*, Roger McGough and Michael Rosen, London, Penguin (Puffin), 1979; *All Sorts of Poems*, Ann Thwaite (ed.), London, Methuen (Magnet), 1978.

To these can be added those anthologies which include teaching ideas: *Writing Poems*, Michael Harrison and Christopher Stuart-Clark, London, Oxford University Press, 1985; *African Poetry for Schools*, Book 1, Noel Machin (ed.), London, Longman, 1978; *Does It Have to Rhyme?*, Sandy Brownjohn, London, Hodder & Stoughton, 1980; *What Rhymes With Secret?* Sandy Brownjohn, London, Hodder & Stoughton, 1982; *Word games* and *More Word Games*, both by Sandy Brownjohn and Janet Whitaker,

London, Hodder & Stoughton, both 1985 (both these started life as much-praised BBC schools radio series); *Not 'Daffodils' Again! Teaching Poetry 9–13*, Schools Council Programme 2, Kenyon Calthrop and Janet Ede (eds), London, Longman, 1984.

Those poems listed can be found in the following anthologies: *A First Poetry Book*, J. Foster (ed.): 'The Quarrel' (p.26), 'Hurry Home' (p.14), 'In the Dark' (p.21), 'Alone in the Grange' (p.94), 'Cold Feet' (p.116); *A Second Poetry Book*, J. Foster (ed.): 'Me' (p.8), 'Why?' (p.123); *A Third Poetry Book*, J. Foster (ed.): 'The Alien' (p.8); *I Like That Stuff*, M. Styles (ed.): 'Happy Birthday, Dilroy' (p.11), 'In Trouble' (p.18); *Speaking to You*, M. Rosen and D. Jackson (eds): 'My Dad These Days' (p.100), 'The Production Line' (p.99), 'Madam and the Census Man' (p.80), 'Agatha's Trousers' (p.76), 'A Working Mum' (p.71), 'School' (p.21), 'First Day at School' (p.18); *African Poetry for Schools*, Noel Machin (ed.), 'Madam and Her Madam' (p.57), 'The Cunjah Man' (p.51), 'Me, Coloured' (p.46, Book 2).

30 Those poems listed can be found in the following anthologies: *A First Poetry Book*, J. Foster (ed.), op. cit.: 'A Centipede' (p.72); *A Second Poetry Book*, J. Foster (ed.), op. cit.: 'Gran' (p.18), 'Night Starvation or the Biter Bit' (p.23), 'Baby Sardine' (p.50); *A Third Poetry Book*, J. Foster (ed.), op. cit.: 'The Haunted Lift' (p.39); *A Fourth Poetry Book*, J. Foster (ed.), op. cit.: 'The Ying-tong-iddle-I-po' (p.40); *I Like That Stuff*, M. Styles (ed.), op. cit.: 'Only the Moon' (p.70); *African Poetry for Schools*, N. Machin (ed.), op. cit.: 'Lullaby' (p.1); *All Sorts of Poems*, A Thwaite (ed.), op. cit.: 'The Headless Gardener' (p.93); *Writing Poems*, M. Harrison and C. Stuart-Clark (eds), op. cit: 'Rabbit in Mixer Survives' (p.81).

Chapter 6   Drama and language development

1   T. Stabler, *Drama in Primary Schools*, Schools Council Drama 5–11 Project, London, Macmillan Education, 1978.
2   Ibid., p.177.
3   Ibid., p.177.
4   Department of Education and Science, *Primary Education in England: A Survey by HM Inspectors of Schools*, London, HMSO, 1978, p.47.
5   Department of Education and Science, *A Language for Life* (The Bullock Report), London, HMSO, 1975, p.156.
6   Stabler, op. cit., p.7.
7   The Bullock Report, op. cit., p.158.
8   See, for example, 'Bandalee' in Philip S. Sherlock's *Anansi the Spider Man*, London, Macmillan Caribbean, 1956.

Suggestions for further reading

Given the huge number of relevant texts which might be recommended at this point, this selection is restricted to those which I, my students, and class teacher colleagues have found particularly helpful and interesting.

Chapter 1   English and the primary school curriculum

Schools Council Working Paper 75, *Primary Practice*, London, Methuen Educational, 1983. This is a businesslike working document intended for all those with an interest in primary education. It considers each of the major curriculum areas, and associated organizational issues, in turn and includes carefully documented examples of good practice.

Joan Dean, *Organizing Learning in the Primary School Classroom*, London, Croom Helm, 1983. This is a thoroughly practical guide for all those who are intent on facilitating learning in the primary classroom through enlightened curriculum and classroom management. In a way which is typical of the author's other works, it combines wisdom with a realistic understanding of the nature, and problems of classrooms.

Robin Alexander, *Primary Teaching*, London, Holt, Rinehart & Winston, 1984. This stimulating book challenges all those involved in primary education to reappraise the assumptions which commonly underpin primary practice.

P534 Course Team, *Every Child's Language*, Book 1, Open University INSET, London, Open University, 1985. This in-service pack for primary teachers looks at key aspects of the language curriculum through a series of short essays, many of which pay particular attention to language diversity and bilingualism in the primary classroom. Book 2, *Case Studies*, records a wide range of projects, which span the primary curriculum and age range. A number of the case studies valuably focus on parental involvement in children's language work, and on ways of supporting bilingual children.

David Houlton, *All Our Languages: A Handbook for the Multilingual Classroom*, London, Edward Arnold, 1985. Although this practical handbook emerged from the Schools Council Mother Tongue Project and is of particular relevance to all those teaching bilingual children, it has much to offer all those who are intent on encouraging a respect for linguistic diversity, whatever the context and wherever the classroom.

Chapter 2   Reading for meaning

Helen Arnold, *Listening to Children Reading*, London, Hodder & Stoughton, 1982. This practical and persuasive book critically appraises typical 'reading aloud' practices in the classroom, and suggests how primary teachers can best exploit reading aloud for a number of different purposes.

Muriel Somerfield, Mike Torbe and Colin Ward, *A Framework for Reading: Creating a Policy in the Primary School*, London, Heinemann, 1983. The nature of this useful text owes much to its pedigree: it evolved from in-service work, discussions with teachers, and observed good practice in the teaching of reading. It is a practical and enlightened guide which is of use to all those interested in reading, and an invaluable aid for those aiming to formulate a language policy within the primary school.

Mary Hoffman, Rob Jeffcoate, Janet Maybin and Neil Mercer, *Children, Language and Literature*, P530 CB, Open University INSET, London, Open University Press, 1982. This collection of short, well-illustrated studies challenges the reader to reassess his own views and knowledge of children's literature, contains case studies which focus on literature in the classroom, and suggests guidelines for those choosing children's books.

Moira McKenzie, *Learning to Read and Reading*, ILEA Curriculum Guideline, London, ILEA, 1979 and Aidan Warlow, *Extending Reading in the Junior School*, ILEA Curriculum Guideline, 1979. These two booklets contribute to a series of personal statements written by ILEA staff concerned with language in the primary school. They are helpful, succinct and well-illustrated.

Hilary Hester, *Stories in the Multilingual Primary School*, London,

ILEA, 1983. This well-illustrated handbook contains many practical and interesting suggestions for exploiting stories. Despite its title, it has relevance for all primary teachers.

Liz Waterland, *Read With Me, An Apprenticeship Approach to Reading*, Thimble Press, London, 1985. Vital reading for all those who feel, like the author, 'There must be a better way . . .' than the reading scheme.

Chapter 3   Writing: processes and purposes, and Chapter 4 Routes into writing

Roger Beard, *Children's Writing in the Primary School*, London, Hodder & Stoughton, 1984. This text dovetails theory and practice effectively to suggest intelligent and practical ways of encouraging a range of classroom writing.

Frank Smith, *Writing and the Writer*, London, Heinemann, 1982. This important work persuasively, and sometimes contentiously, considers the processes involved in writing, reading and learning. Significantly, it draws the reader into the situation which faces the young writer, and forces the teacher to recognize the arbitrary and unnecessary classroom constraints which make an already difficult task even more fearsome. Interesting, sometimes fascinating, always challenging.

Lucy McCormish Calkins, *Lessons from a Child: On the Teaching and Learning of Writing*, London, Heinemann, 1983. This slim book chronicles the writing development of Susie, a third grade pupil in an American elementary school, but in the process shows how class teacher and researcher came to modify the week, the curriculum, the classroom, and their ideas, in order to help children to write at will and at length. The book acknowledges its debt to the pioneering work of Donald Murray and Donald Graves.

Chapter 5   A place for poetry

Please refer to the Reference section for recommended works.

Chapter 6   Drama and language development

Paul Ratledge, *The Waste Ground: Learning through Drama*, London, ILEA, 1984. This pack of materials provides an excellent introduction to educational drama in practice, in the primary school. It demonstrates how drama can be used as a medium for language development and learning, in this case about the local community. The pack is full of practical ideas, and usefully considers a number of key drama techniques.

Tom Stabler, *Drama in Primary Schools*, Schools Council Drama 5–11 Project, London, Macmillan Education, 1978. This project report goes beyond the mere recording of survey findings to present teachers of drama at work, in sometimes less than ideal conditions. It is a useful guide for those looking for a coherent rationale for educational drama, and for those seeking practical ways of introducing drama into the primary curriculum.

Index

Index